The Noon book of authentic
Indian cookery

The Noon book of authentic
Indian cookery

G K Noon

Foreword by
Delia Smith

HarperCollins*Publishers*

Foreword

I have known Noon (no-one knows him as anything else) for ten years and it's thanks to him that I once – for the only time in my life – cheated on my dinner guests. Hidden in the kitchen were a variety of packs of his wonderful, factory-made curries. I didn't actually claim dinner was home-made, but my guests assumed it was and at the end I got embarrassing and very genuine compliments on the flavour and authenticity of the meal. It was all done in the cause of research for an article and when you see the quality, care and inventiveness that go into Noon's production process, you can understand why such praise is entirely deserved.

To have created authenticity in his ready-meal range – spices are bought whole by the ton and roasted precisely and to order – is Noon's abiding achievement. This book takes us even further, on a first-hand journey through the regions and cultures of India, to bring in the dazzling flavours of the sub-continent in classic dishes and in lesser known local specialities. All of them make you want to go straight to the kitchen and start grinding a few spices, and all of them carry Noon's trademark – authenticity.

Delia Smith

Introduction G.K. Noon

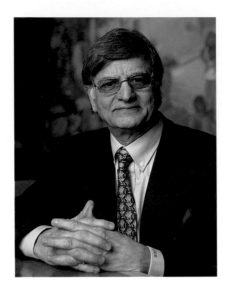

I have spent my entire working life in the food business – and it has left me hungry for more! My mother was an excellent cook and I can still remember the aroma of her Indian and Persian cooking – her family came from Shiraz in Iran. I especially remember the prawns that she bought fresh which she then peeled; she was a discerning woman who placed great emphasis on good food and good company.

I am passionate about food and enjoy nothing better than to cook for a group of friends. I am delighted to share my enthusiasm for Indian food with you through the recipes in this book. They are authentic recipes that my mother would have recognised were she still alive. Each recipe has been perfected by the chefs at Noon Products, and it is recipes such as these that have helped fuel the growth of our company. They are tried and tested and easy to use.

Indian food is immensely popular in this country. A walk through the chilled food aisles of British supermarkets is revealing. It shows just how many distinct Indian regional cuisines have become familiar to the British consumer. With the demands of increasingly well-travelled and sophisticated consumers in mind, the master chefs at Noon can spend up to six months developing a single recipe. Each recipe reflects its provenance in the authentic ingredients and cooking methods used.

This book offers a wide cross-section of Indian food, from the Moghlai cuisine of North India and the vegetarian delights of Madras, to the fish specialities of the Malabar Coast, and many others. I hope you will enjoy the adventure of cooking them in your own kitchen. It's a slice of India that I am sure you will relish. Enjoy cooking.

The Noon chefs, from left to right:

B. Sainath Rao
Puneet Arora
Rakesh Yadav
Mr Ashok Kaul
Vishal Rew
Sumit Malik

Contents

Map of India	8
Regions of India	9
Menu Planning	14
Flavours and Textures	16
Herbs and Spices	18
Pulses and Grains	20
Basics of Indian Cooking	22
Kashmir	26
Moghlai	38
Tandoor	54
Bengal	64
Mumbai	76
Goa	88
Hyderabad	100
Chennai	112
Breads, Chutneys and Sweets	126
Glossary	140
Index	141
Credits	143

KASHMIR

DELHI ●

BENGAL

● CALCUTTA

MUMBAI
(Bombay) ●

● HYDERABAD

Bay of Bengal

GOA

Arabian
Sea

● CHENNAI
(Madras)

Regions of India

by Mohini Kent

If what we eat describes who we are, then India is a baffling place, its menus dictated by the vagaries of history, caste, community, religion and region.

Indian history is a long litany of strange names – Dravidian, Aryan, Buddhist, Greek, Muslim, Parsee, Sikh, Portuguese, French, Dutch and English names – a story of migration, of blood and greed, of conquest and intrigue, of evangelical missionaries and moral crusaders. Even men of God who built empires of the spirit have helped to shape the cuisine. The country is the world's biggest food bazaar.

The Indian landscape too is a study in contrasts. From the highest mountain in the world, the Everest, to the dry, arid desert of Rajasthan, lush jungles and long, tropical coastlines, the local availability of green vegetables, grains, meat and fish have helped to mould eating habits as much as religious taboo. There are those who eat only wheat and others who eat only rice; some cook in *ghee* (clarified butter) but others use only coconut oil. Northerners drink tea from Assam but in the south they drink coffee from the great estates of Coorg and Ooty.

Legend has it that the first immigrants to India, the Dravidians, arrived about 9000 B.C. from a land that sank into the sea. Then, between the 4th and 2nd millennium B.C., came the Aryans, a semi-nomadic, pastoral people who lived chiefly on the produce of the sacred cow and for whom eating beef was taboo.

South India

The lighter-skinned Aryans pushed the dark-skinned Dravidians south of the Vindhya mountain range that neatly divides India into two. In the south, Tamil cities such as Chennai (formerly Madras) on the eastern Coromandel Coast preserved Dravidian culture and great temples grew into centres of the arts such as sculpture and the classical Bharata Natyam dance. Rice and dal (lentils) remain at the heart of their cuisine – although it is by no means all vegetarian. The climate is hot – and then it gets hotter! – and food is spicy.

On the western Malabar coast, St Thomas the Apostle is believed to have arrived some years after the death of Jesus and converted India's first Christians. Centuries later, the Portuguese brought their own, more brutal, Catholicism to the coast, followed by the Dutch, Loreto and Carmelite nuns, and large communities of Christians still live there. It was the dream of William Wilberforce, the

traders and ship-builders who built ships for the
English during the Napoleonic wars. The
Parsees have no inhibitions about diet, although
they abstain from eating beef out of respect for
Hindus, and their cooking represents a fusion of
Persian and Indian, their most famous dish
being *dhansak* (meat with lentils). The
pomegranate, symbol of fertility, and the date,
symbolic of the tree of life, are included in
Parsee feasts in memory of their days in Iran,
but the rice, fish and coconut in their food are
distinctly Indian additions.

The Portuguese Vasco de Gama arrived in
Calicut on the Malabar Coast in 1498 A.D.
looking for 'christians and spices'. A decade
later the Portuguese had captured Goa and there
they stayed until 1961. In religion, the
Portuguese were intolerant and mass
conversions by Franciscan and Jesuit
missionaries have left Goa half-catholic.
Portuguese married local women after
converting them, a strategy intended to produce
a large Portuguese-Catholic population. All
things Portuguese were highly prized, including
olives and olive oil. Now Goa is a good mix of
Hindu, Muslim and Portuguese culture.
Different ingredients and different cooking
methods distinguish the cuisine of one
community from another. For example, Goans
of Portuguese Catholic descent will use vinegar
and eat roast suckling pig whilst Goan Hindus
prefer to use tamarind or lime juice as souring
agents and prefer to eat chicken or mutton. Both
communities relish the plentiful fish.

Kerala, in the very south of India, is also
home to the traditional system of Ayurveda that
uses herbal medicine to cure illness. It is a
holistic approach, recognising the role of the
mind in healing the body and the dynamic play
of the three elements of fire, water and air in the
individual. Ayurveda doctors use herbs and
spices to bring about that balance in the body
necessary for optimum health.

anti-slavery campaigner, to convert the whole of
India to Christianity, but they remain about
3 percent of the population. Their cuisine has
developed according to local taste but, since they
have few or no taboos, it is quite distinct. For
example, *appam*, the rice pancake of Kerala,
would be eaten with *aviyal* (vegetables in coconut
milk) by the Hindu Nair community but the
Syrian Christians could eat it with beef stew.

The earliest Jews came to India in ancient
times but the Cochin Jews arrived in the 1st
century A.D., fleeing persecution by the
Romans. Their numbers have dwindled through
migration and the synagogue at Cochin has not
had a rabbi in living memory. Indian Jews
observe the dietary restrictions of the Old
Testament, including the ban on pork and the
injunction to eat kosher meat. Orthodox Jews
eat meat and dairy products in separate meals,
even using different pans for each.

The Parsees, the Zoroastrians of Persia,
arrived in the 8th century A.D. in Gujarat, in the
far west, spreading later to Bombay. They were

North India

In the north is the Hindu holy city of Benaras, the city of Lord Shiva, one of the supreme Gods of the holy Hindu trinity. Shiva's consort is Annapoorna, the Goddess of food. Food acquires great ritual significance in a Hindu's life: at birth, an infant's head is rubbed with ghee; six months later comes the ritual of Annaprasna when a baby tastes his first solid food; sweets are auspicious so boxes of sweetmeats are exchanged on happy occasions such as festivals, births and marriages; widows are forbidden from eating 'heating' foods such as onions and garlic, also shunned by some ascetics. Even the soul of the dead receives food offerings, called pinda-daan. A Hindu's life is traditionally divided into four stages of learning and knowledge; marriage and parenthood; the beginning of detachment from the world (when one's children are married), leading to total renunciation, and there is food prescribed for each stage. Throughout life, the stomach should only be half full of food, leaving it half empty, a quarter for water and a quarter for the movement of air to aid digestion.

Each caste, community and sect of Hinduism has its own food etiquette and taboos, which were partly designed to maintain caste purity, but these are breaking down, particularly in the big cities, as are the distinctly different cuisines of different religious communities. Earlier, people ate only at home; now, hotels and restaurants often serve a homogenised cuisine with some regional specialities.

Benaras lies on the banks of the sacred river Ganges – orthodox Hindus prefer to drink only Ganges water and erstwhile maharajas carried it abroad in large silver urns – and the rich delta yields a cornucopia of grains, vegetables and fruit, including mangoes. At the gates of ancient Benaras lay Sarnath, where the Buddha came to preach his first sermon in the 6th century B.C.

The Buddha preached the Middle Path of non-violence and compassion and his injunction against killing any living being gave the impetus to vegetarianism. Three hundred years later, Emperor Ashoka made Buddhism the state religion, banned hunting and turned vegetarian. The priestly class followed his example and even today the Brahmin caste tends to be vegetarian whereas lower castes tend to be meat-eaters.

The inhospitable Thar desert of Rajasthan, in the north west, challenged man's culinary creativity. Water was scarce, green vegetables rare, imported rice a luxury. The Marwaris of Rajasthan dried *sangri*, a thorny plant, in the sun and the whip-like fronds had to be soaked for several hours before cooking. Potatoes were a rarity, *bajra* the staple grain and dry red chillies from Jaipur freely used. Pickles livened up a limited meal.

The kings of the desert were keen *shikaris* (hunters) and game cooking developed into a fine art. For example, *sule* was made with venison, wild boar or sand grouse and *khad* was a layered dish, made with chappatis and meat,

taster would taste everything. Harem ladies wore the finest clothes and ate exotic food brought from great distances. Abul Fazal, historian of Emperor Akbar's reign, describes the extravagant grocery shopping list and the lavish meals. For example, ducks, waterfowl and some vegetables came from Kashmir – as did blocks of ice. Sheep, goat and fowl were especially fattened up – fowls were never kept for less than a month before being slaughtered. High standards were kept up even when the emperor was on the move and living in camps.

Apart from the Moghul kingdom, India had several other important Muslim kingdoms, such as Hyderabad, Awadh and Rampur, although it is Moghlai cuisine that has become internationally popular.

originally baked in a hole in the ground with charcoal and hot sand.

Delhi and the Moghuls

The Arabs had long been coming to India in their dhows to trade but in 1000 A.D. the first Muslim invader from Afghanistan defeated the northern Hindu king. For almost a thousand years, Delhi was ruled by Muslims – first by sultans of Arab origin and then the Great Moghul emperors. Islam, with its prohibition on pork and emphasis on eating only jhatka/kosher meat, had its own impact on India, particularly through Moghlai cuisine.

Babar, a conqueror from near Samarkand, defeated the Muslim sultan of Delhi at the Battle of Panipat in 1526 A.D. and, for the next 300 years, his family ruled north India, first from Agra, location of the famous Taj Mahal, then from Delhi. The Moghuls took their cultural cue from Persia, adding nuts, saffron and cream to the cuisine that existed in India. The emperors ate only in the harem because of the threat of poisoning. Over a hundred dishes were prepared for the emperor at each meal. Dishes were locked and sealed in the kitchen and the seal broken in the emperor's presence, where a food

The Punjab

The magnificent maharajas developed their own culinary styles. The Sikh Maharajas of Patiala, in the northern state of Punjab, enjoyed the fine things of life, including wine and food, and their kitchens were famous. Patiala, for example, employed 35 master chefs, each of whom specialised in only one dish, for example potatoes, and they had about 200 assistants. Punjab is the breadbasket of India. Its rich soil, watered by the famous five rivers, yields abundant harvests of wheat and corn, mustard and sugar-cane and a large variety of vegetables. Milk, yogurt and *ghee* are consumed in vast quantities. Sikhism was founded in Punjab in the 15th century by Guru Nanak, who preached a quietist, pacifist faith that reconciled the warring religions of Hinduism and Islam. Nine spiritual gurus followed Guru Nanak and it was the tenth Guru Gobind Singh who gave Sikhs their distinct identity. An important aspect of the faith is the free kitchen at the *gurudwara* (sikh temple) where any one, irrespective of caste or creed, can enjoy a free meal. Wheat halwa called *kadha prashad* is given as blessed food. The use of tobacco is strictly forbidden, as is beef. Sikhs make up about 2 percent of the population and live mainly in Punjab, Haryana and Delhi.

Anglo-India

The last invaders of India – after the Greeks, Turks, Arabs, Moghuls, Portuguese and French – were the English. They came for spices but saw rich pickings and stayed to take over the empire of the Great Moghuls. At first, Calcutta, in the north east, was the capital and the existing clubs, the Tollygunge, the Saturday Club, the Calcutta Club, still reek of the Raj. Kippers for breakfast were imported from England but at Christmas pea-fowl was sometimes served in place of turkey. The clubs of the Raj existed in every civil and military station: the Ooty Club is an imposing Regency building, its walls lined with tiger skins, bison heads and portraits of former viceroys. The Madras Clubhouse is an imposing 18th-century mansion and Bombay's Willingdon Sports Club and the Royal Bombay Yacht Club survive intact. What is striking about the clubs is their Englishness. Menus still offer puddings such as souffles, trifles and steamed pudding.

The British inspired the ubiquitous cutlet, now to be found on most Indian railway stations and trains. Other British culinary legacies to India are the toast and some desserts, both 'nursery' puddings and others. If what they left behind is meagre, what they took away with them when they left India in 1947 is a great deal more and makes a far more interesting story.

Today, Indian 'curry' has become a British national dish. British housewives can now pick up tandoori dishes, kormas, Goan fish curry and dozens of other authentic dishes in supermarkets as part of their weekly shopping. Queen Victoria would have approved. She wanted Indian food but when her Swiss chef served up an unpalatable mix of curry powder

and water, thickened with plenty of flour, the queen revolted. Then she appointed an Indian servant, Abdul Karim, to cook the royal family authentic curries. Karim became her confidante, taught her Hindustani and was known as 'The Munshi'.

Now the story of Indian food, as colourful as a spice market, as 'chat-patta' as a plate of *bhel-poori*, has grown and grown, becoming a tale told in many tongues across the world's continents.

Menu Planning

Traditional Indian meals combine meats (optional), grains, pulses, vegetables, milk products (yoghurt, paneer, etc.) and sweets (dessert) to provide a well balanced diet.

Vegetarian lunch menu

Mulagu-tanni *114*
A coconut and apple flavoured chickpea soup.

❖ ❖ ❖

Saag paneer *50*
A combination of fresh spinach and paneer with a hint of garlic.

Tamatar, phool gobi, muttar che saar *84*
Cauliflower and peas cooked together in a tomato-flavoured tangy masala.

Madras potato *124*
A fiery potato dish from southern India.

Kadhai chholey *53*
Chickpeas tossed in an onion-tomato masala, flavoured with a blend of spices.

Gucchi pulao *133*
Fragrant basmati rice and morel mushroms cooked together with aromatic spices.

Naan / parantha / chutneys *128–33*
Assorted Indian breads and chutneys.

❖ ❖ ❖

Aam phirni *137*
Traditional Indian dessert made with mangoes, rice and milk.

Seviyan *139*
Fine vermicelli cooked in milk and scented with cardamoms.

Non-vegetarian lunch menu

Chicken cafrael *97*
Traditional Goan delicacy of chicken, marinated in a spicy green paste and then deep-fried.

❖ ❖ ❖

Jheenga charchari *66*
A delicacy from Calcutta…prawns stir-fried in pickling spices and garlic.

Nilgiri korma *116*
Lamb simmered in a gravy made of fresh greens and flavoured with home-made spice mixture.

Vanghi *87*
Baby aubergines cooked in a paste made with jaggery, onions and tamarind and spiced with 'goda masala'.

Sambhar *119*
A south Indian lentil dal with fresh vegetables.

Sesame rice *123*
Sesame-flavoured basmati rice.

Naan / parantha / chutneys *128–33*
Assorted Indian breads and chutneys.

❖ ❖ ❖

Kheer *137*
A light dessert made with basmati rice, milk and nuts.

Shrikhand *135*
An unusual dessert, made with hung yoghurt, sugar and green cardamom, garnished with nuts.

Vegetarian dinner menu

Thakkali rassam 115

*Essence of tomatoes, enhanced with asafoetida, curry leaves
and crushed black pepper.*

❖ ❖ ❖

Subz kebab 62

*Seasonal vegetables marinated, grilled and served
on a skewer.*

❖ ❖ ❖

Shobjee jhalfarezi 75

*Assorted vegetables stir-fried in pickling spices
and coconut.*

Baghare baingan 109

*A Hyderabadi speciality of aubergines cooked
in a gravy made of roasted onions, sesame seeds, jaggery
and coconut.*

Rajma 34

Red kidney beans, Kashmiri style, with ginger and yoghurt.

Saag dal 111

*A delicious combination of baby spinach and gram lentils
with a hint of lemon juice.*

Tarkari biryani 46

Fresh seasonal vegetables cooked with fragrant basmati rice.

Poori / parantha / naan / roti / chutneys

128–33

Assorted Indian breads and chutneys.

❖ ❖ ❖

Kheer 137

A light dessert made with basmati rice, milk and nuts.

Shahi tukra 139

*Dessert for royalty…deep fried bread soaked in perfumed milk
and covered with reduced milk.*

Non-vegetarian dinner menu

Murg shorba 40

Chicken soup flavoured with onion and cumin seeds and garlic.

❖ ❖ ❖

Achari bateyr 49

Quails cooked in a onion-tomato masala.

❖ ❖ ❖

Prawn balchao 99

*A Goan speciality of prawns in a fiery tomato masala with
black pepper, cloves, cinnamon and fennel.*

Dum ka murg 47

Chicken delicacy cooked in a sealed vessel with mild spices.

Dum aloo 36

*A Kashmiri speciality of potatoes simmered in yoghurt
and spices.*

Tamatar, phool gobi, muttar che saar 84

Cauliflower and peas in a tomato-flavoured tangy masala.

Cabbage poriyal 124

*Shredded cabbage stir-fried with coconut, mustard seeds,
green coriander, lemon, garlic and crisp-fried lentil.*

Lamb biryani 52

Lamb cooked with fragrant basmati rice and aromatic spices.

Poori / parantha / naan / roti / chutneys

128–33

Assorted Indian breads and chutneys.

❖ ❖ ❖

Aam phirni 137

Traditional Indian dessert made with mangoes, rice and milk.

Shahi tukra 139

*Dessert for the royalty…deep fried bread soaked in perfumed
milk and covered with reduced milk.*

Flavours and Textures

Capturing the flavours and textures of Indian food is as complex as trying to describe the myriad patterns and weaves of regional saris because dishes too vary in appearance, texture and taste from region to region.

North Indian Punjabi curries are traditionally rich in texture and heavy with ghee, butter or cream, because that is needed to withstand the cold North Indian winters. Vegetables, too, are slow-cooked in thick onion-based gravy. *Mattar paneer*, for example, is a rich dish of fried cottage cheese cooked with peas in a curry of onions, tomatoes and spices, with a dash of yogurt. Cooking time is long so that flavours are released slowly.

Thick curries go well with Indian bread such as wheat *chappatis*, *pooris*, *kulchas*, *naan* and tandoori *roti*. Dry, roasted tandoori meat is marinated for at least six hours before cooking. The tandoor provides wrap-around heat, one of the most effective ways of roasting, and it gives the meat the familiar smoked charcoal flavour.

Bengalis, on the other hand, tend to cook thin fish curries that are more suitable for eating with rice. The popular mustard oil gives dishes a sharp flavour but food is not highly spiced and fresh ginger is widely used. Further north-east, in Assam and Darjeeling, food is often steamed, and some of the world's best tea comes from the great estates there.

The flavours of the desert are robust and food is hot, using the dry red chillies of Jasdan. Game is cooked on open spits or, in parts of Rajasthan, raw meat with whole spices is buried in containers in the hot sand to cook in natural heat, becoming so tender that the meat comes off the bone.

Gujaratis tend to add some sugar to most dishes and they make heavy use of the *sil-batta* (grinding stone) to make masala paste for cooking or for making the legion of fresh chutneys they serve with snacks.

A good tip is to use masala as fresh as possible. Stale garam masala, for example, will not have much flavour, and it is important to use fresh ginger, garlic and green coriander. The sequential steps in cooking Indian food are vital and should be followed as given in the recipe. Dry spices burn easily and, if this happens, it is better to throw away a batch and start again rather than risk ruining the dish.

It is important to understand spices and their use. Asafoetida, for example, can be used in place of garlic. Inept cooks confuse the palate with dishes that taste of everything all at once, but master chefs use spices skilfully to give each dish a particular flavour. For example, if the dominant note is of green cardamom then the rest of the spices are subdued and only those are used that complement that particular flavour.

Herbs and Spices

Herbs and spices should be used to heighten the taste and flavour of the main ingredient in a recipe and should never be overpowering. Use only the freshest herbs, and grind spices as you need them – they soon lose their flavour once ground.

1 Dried red chillies
2 Fresh chillies
3 Bay leaves
4 Fresh coriander leaves
5 Curry leaves
6 Stone flower (lichen)
7 Vetiver roots
8 Cinnamon (cassia) bark

9 Nigella seeds
10 Cloves
11 Ground ginger
12 Turmeric
13 Cumin seeds
14 Fennel seeds
15 Coriander seeds
16 Saffron strands
17 Garlic
18 Green cardamom pods
19 Fresh ginger

Pulses and Grains

India is predominantly a vegetarian nation and pulses and grains are therefore an important element of the cuisine. The variety grown is astounding, and many are used fresh, rather than the dried varieties we are used to in this country.

1 Brown rice
2 Basmati rice
3 Goan red rice
4 Yellow split peas (chana dal)
5 Mung split lentils

6 Red chori lentils
7 Green mung beans
8 Urid whole or black lentils
9 Green lentils
10 Shelled urid lentils
11 Red kidney beans
12 Whole brown lentils (urad dal)
13 Split red lentils

Basics of Indian Cooking

These basic mixtures are used time and again in Indian cookery. If necessary, increase the quantities given below as specified in individual recipes.

Ginger Purée

Put 50g/2oz peeled and chopped ginger in a blender or food processor with 1 tablespoon of water and process to a smooth purée. It will keep in the fridge for 2–3 days.

Garlic Purée

Put 50g/2oz peeled and chopped garlic in a blender or food processor with 1 tablespoon of water and process to a smooth purée. It will keep in the fridge for 2–3 days.

Green Chilli Purée

Put 50g/2oz green chillies in a blender or food processor with 1 tablespoon of water and process to a smooth purée. It will keep in the fridge for 2–3 days.

Raw Onion Purée

Put 50g/2oz peeled and chopped raw onion in a blender or food processor with 1 tablespoon of water and process to a smooth purée. It will keep in the fridge for 2–3 days.

Fried Onion Purée

Deep-fry thinly sliced onions in moderately hot oil until they turn golden brown. Drain on kitchen paper to absorb excess oil. Put the fried onions in a blender or food processor with an equal volume of water and process to a smooth paste. It will keep in the fridge for about 1 week. Alternatively, the fried onions can be stored in an airtight container in the fridge, and the paste can be made as and when required.

Cashew Nut Paste

Put 50g/2oz cashew nuts in a blender or food processor with 4 tablespoons of water and process to a fine paste. It will keep in the fridge for 2–3 days.

Ghee

Put 1 litre/1¾ pints double cream in a heavy-based pan and bring to the boil. Simmer for about 25 minutes, until all the moisture has evaporated, stirring frequently to prevent sticking. Once all the moisture has evaporated, the mixture should become clear. Stop stirring and let the sediment settle at the bottom, but don't let it burn. Remove from the heat and leave for 5 minutes, then strain through a muslin-lined sieve.

Clarified Butter

Melt 250g/9oz unsalted butter in a heavy-based pan, then simmer over a very low heat for about 10 minutes, until all the froth has settled and the butter becomes clear. Remove from the heat and leave for 3–5 minutes to allow the sediment to settle. Skim any impurities from the top, then gently pour off the clarified butter, leaving the sediment in the base of the pan.

Curry Powder

2 tablespoons ground turmeric
2 tablespoons ground cumin
1 tablespoon red chilli powder
4 tablespoons ground coriander
¹/₂ teaspoon asafoetida
¹/₄ teaspoon ground fenugreek seeds

1 Mix all the spices together and store in an airtight container in a cool, dry place. The curry powder will keep for up to a month.

Chat Masala Powder

This is a proprietary spice mixture, available at Indian stores. It is a tangy, spicy, slightly sweet and salty blend of spices that is used to sprinkle onto the finished dish (especially dry dishes), or sometimes included in the dish. Common ingredients are dried ginger, black salt, carom seed, black pepper, black cardamom, green cardamom, cumin, dried mint, fenugreek leaves, dried mango, asafoetida, red chilli and cloves.

Always use fresh herb or vegetable purées immediately after grinding to obtain maximum flavour.

Masalas, as these mixes are known, are always made in different ways, every person making their own particular blend of spices. Use within 2 weeks for maximum flavour.

Garam Masala

20g/³/₄oz green cardamom
   pods
25g/1oz black cardamom
   pods
1¹/₂ teaspoons cloves
7 cinnamon sticks (2.5cm/
   1 inch long)

5 bay leaves
2 mace blades
25g/1oz black peppercorns
25g/1oz cumin seeds
25g/1oz coriander seeds
15g/¹/₂oz fennel seeds
¹/₂ nutmeg

1 Dry-roast all the spices except the nutmeg in a heavy-based frying pan over a medium heat for 10 minutes.

2 Grind them in a spice grinder, then grate in the nutmeg and leave to cool. Store in an airtight container in a cool, dry place.

Chholey Masala

50g/2oz coriander seeds
50g/2oz dried mango powder
2 teaspoons black salt
15g/¹/₂oz dried pomegranate
   seeds
10 dried red chillies
15g/¹/₂oz cumin seeds
15g/¹/₂oz green cardamom
   pods
1 teaspoon black peppercorns

4–5 fenugreek seeds
¹/₄ teaspoon cloves
¹/₄ teaspoon cassia buds
6–8 cinnamon sticks
a pinch of carom seeds
a pinch of freshly grated
   nutmeg
¹/₂ teaspoon ground ginger
a pinch of ground mace

1 Dry-roast all the ingredients except the nutmeg, ginger and mace in a heavy-based frying pan over a low heat for 10–15 minutes.

2 Grind in a spice grinder, then stir in the nutmeg, ginger and mace and leave to cool. Store in an airtight container in a cool, dry place.

Goda Masala

This blend of spices is used in western India. It should be stirred in towards the end of cooking, as all the spices are already roasted. If it is added at the beginning, not only will it lose its flavour but it will make the dish black in appearance.

1 Dry-roast the first 10 ingredients in a heavy-based pan over a low heat for 10–15 minutes, until they give off their aroma. Remove from the pan and set aside. Dry-roast the coconut until golden.

2 Put the coconut and roasted spices in a spice grinder and grind to a fine powder, then stir in the turmeric, asafoetida and stoneflower. Leave to cool.

3 Store in an airtight container in a cool dry place.

50g/2oz coriander seeds
1 teaspoon cumin seeds
¹/₂ teaspoon black cumin seeds
¹/₃ teaspoon black peppercorns
2–3 dried red chillies
5–6 cloves
1 cinnamon stick
2 bay leaves
2 tablespoons sesame seeds
¹/₃ teaspoon cassia buds
3 tablespoons desiccated
   coconut
¹/₂ teaspoon ground turmeric
a pinch of asafoetida
a pinch of stoneflower

Sambhar Powder

This blend of spices is used in southern Indian cooking and varies from region to region.

1 tablespoon groundnut oil
1¹/₂ teaspoons channa dal (yellow split peas)
1¹/₂ teaspoons urad dal (black gram beans)
1 tablespoon coriander seeds
2 teaspoons cumin seeds
1 teaspoon black peppercorns
1 teaspoon mustard seeds
1 teaspoon fenugreek seeds
3 dried red chillies
¹/₂ teaspoon ground turmeric
a generous pinch of asafoetida

1 Heat the oil in a frying pan, add the channa dal and urad dal and fry over a low heat until they turn golden brown. Remove from the pan and drain on kitchen paper to absorb excess oil.

2 Put all the ingredients, including the dal, into a spice grinder and grind to a fine powder. Store in an airtight container in a cool, dry place.

Achari or Panch Phoran Spice Mix

This spice mix can be used whole for tempering or ground and stored in an airtight container.

25g/1oz cumin seeds
100g/4oz anise seeds
50g/2oz mustard seeds
¹/₂ teaspoon fenugreek seeds
¹/₂ teaspoon onion seeds (nigella seeds)

1 To use the spice mix whole, simply mix all the spices together.

2 For a ground spice mix, dry-roast the spices in a heavy-based frying pan over a low heat for 10–15 minutes. Grind them in a spice grinder and leave to cool. Store in an airtight container in a cool, dry place.

Boondi

This is made from chickpea flour and is usually available in Indian shops. Here's how to make your own.

300g/11oz chickpea flour
a pinch of ground turmeric
¹/₄ teaspoon ground cumin
a pinch of asafoetida
a pinch of baking powder
500ml/17fl oz oil for deep-frying
salt to taste

1 Put all the ingredients except the oil in a bowl, add 3 tablespoons of water and mix together to make a batter. It should have a coating consistency and should not be too thin. Set aside for 30 minutes.

2 Heat the oil over a medium heat. Pour in a little of the batter through a perforated spoon so that it falls into the pan in droplets.

3 Remove the fried balls from the oil just before they start to turn golden brown and drain on kitchen paper. Repeat with the remaining batter. Store in an airtight container in a cool, dry place.

A typical Kashmiri Muslim feast is called a *Wazwan* – a
highly formal meal that consists of 36 courses, of which at
least half are meat dishes

Kashmir

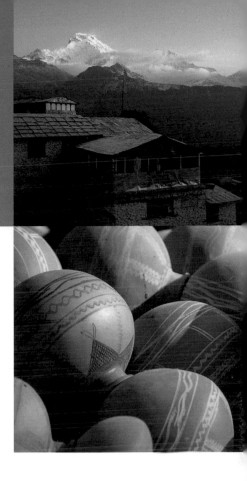

The Moghul Emperor Jahangir said of Kashmir, 'If there is paradise on earth, it is here, it is here, it is here!' The valley of Kashmir, ringed by majestic Himalayan mountains, home to the mountain antelope whose wool is made into the famous pashmina shawls, is a sylvan land of lakes, trees and gardens. Almond trees blossom in March, the chinar is in leaf in April, strawberries and cherries abound in May and apricots follow in June. Autumn brings pears and pomegranates. No wonder Jahangir exclaimed, '*Gar firdaus baruae zami ast; Hamee ast, hamee ast, hamee ast!*'

Like the rest of India, Kashmir has a mixed religious pedigree. Both Buddhism and Hinduism flourished there and Islam arrived in the 14th century, almost two hundred years before Kashmir was conquered by the Moghul Emperor Akbar. Before the advent of Islam, pork was widely eaten. Later, Kashmiri Hindus adopted many elements of Moghul cooking. Brahmins, for example, are generally vegetarian but many Kashmiri Brahmins became meat-eaters. There are some basic differences between the cuisine of Hindu Kashmiri Pandits and Kashmiri Muslims – for example, Hindus generally use yogurt and *hing* (asafoetida) to flavour their food whilst Muslims use onions and garlic. For Hindus, one of the most important festivals is Shivratri, the festival of Lord Shiva, when families both pray and feast together. Navreh, the Kashmiri new year, is welcomed with a thaali piled with rice, yogurt, honey, walnuts and other symbols of prosperity.

Kashmiris use a number of dried vegetables in their cooking, such as turnips, tomatoes, beans, peas and cabbage, grown in summer on the lakes and dried for use in the long, harsh winters when the valley is snow-bound, temperatures drop to -10°C, and Kashmiris carry around individual charcoal fires for warmth. Hot *kahwah* – green tea brewed in samovars with cardamom and almonds – is sipped all day long. Saffron was introduced to Kashmir from Mediterranean countries and is widely used in cooking. Nuts and dried fruit are popular in winter, and both rice and wheat are staples: rice is cooked in many forms, both savoury and sweet; and many types of wheat bread are eaten, such as *kulchas*, *sheermal* and the soft *bakarkhani*.

The Kashmiris eat seated on the floor – as is the custom in India. A piece of cloth called *dastarkhwan* is put on the floor and the food placed on it; people sit around the cloth and eat from plates called *trami*. Each *trami* can hold enough food for 3–4 people, and that is how the food is eaten – by sharing.

Qalia means gravy with the ingredients blended with water.

It is a general term for a lamb or chicken dish in Kashmir.

Qalia

Lamb chops in yoghurt gravy

1 Heat the ghee or clarified butter in a large pan, add the asafoetida, yoghurt, cloves, lamb, chilli powder, ginger purée, ground ginger, fennel seed and some salt. Simmer, uncovered, for 20 minutes, letting the juices from the meat and yoghurt evaporate until a reddish-brown sediment appears. Stir frequently to prevent burning.

2 Scrape up the sediment from the base of the pan, turning the meat frequently until it is brown. Add 100ml/3½fl oz water and cook for 10–15 minutes.

3 Add the turmeric and stir it in well. Add 250ml/8fl oz water and simmer for 15 minutes.

4 Add the potatoes and another 100ml/3½fl oz water, then cover and cook until the meat is tender. The sauce should be thin but not watery.

5 Stir in the garam masala, sugar and chopped coriander.

Serves 4–6

100g/4oz ghee or clarified
  butter (see page 23)
⅛ teaspoon asafoetida
200g/7oz yoghurt, preferably
  Greek yogurt, whisked
4 cloves
1kg/2¼lb double lamb chops
  (i.e. 2 chops joined
  together)
1 teaspoon red chilli powder
1 tablespoon Ginger Purée
  (see page 22)
⅛ teaspoon ground ginger
¼ teaspoon ground fennel
  seed
2 teaspoons ground turmeric
250g/9oz potatoes, peeled and
  cut into 2.5cm/1 inch cubes
1 teaspoon Garam Masala
  (see page 24)
1 tablespoon sugar
4 tablespoons chopped fresh
  coriander
salt to taste

Qalia originated in snowbound areas where, to keep the cold at bay, warm liquids were needed; this soupy dish could be eaten as well as drunk.

Roganjosh is a derivative of *Rogangosht,*

literally meaning lamb curry with saffron-infused oil.

Roganjosh

Lamb curry

Serves 4–6

150ml/¼ pint vegetable oil
4 cloves
3 cinnamon sticks
¼ teaspoon asafoetida
1kg/2¼lb boneless leg of
   lamb, cut into 2.5cm/1 inch
   dice
275g/10oz yoghurt, preferably
   Greek yoghurt, whisked
2 tablespoons Ginger Purée
   (see page 22)
1 tablespoon red chilli powder
½ teaspoon ground ginger

1 tablespoon sugar
1 teaspoon Garam Masala
   (see page 24)
¼ teaspoon saffron strands
4 tablespoons khoya (reduced
   milk) or full-fat milk powder
25g/1oz ground almonds
½ teaspoon bottled vetiver
   water
1 tablespoon finely shredded
   fresh ginger
2 tablespoons fresh coriander
   leaves
salt to taste

1 Heat the oil in a large pan, add the whole spices, asafoetida, lamb, yoghurt, ginger purée, chilli powder and ground ginger. Cover and simmer on a very low heat for 20–25 minutes, until all the juices from the meat and yoghurt evaporate and a reddish-brown sediment begins to appear.

2 Scrape up the sediment from the base of the pan and continue to cook, turning the meat, for about 15 minutes, until the meat turns reddish brown.

3 Add the sugar and some salt to taste, then pour in 250ml/ 8fl oz water. Cover and cook on a very low heat for 20 minutes. Add the garam masala and saffron and cook for another 5 minutes.

4 When the meat is nearly done, add the khoya or milk powder and ground almonds. Cook gently for another 10 minutes, until most of the liquid has been absorbed. Sprinkle over the vetiver water and garnish with the shredded ginger and coriander leaves.

Shab means night and *degh* is the cooking vessel.

As the name suggests, this dish is traditionally cooked overnight.

Shabdegh

Lamb with chilli, ginger and turnips

1 Heat the ghee or clarified butter in a large pan, add the asafoetida, cloves, lamb, chilli powder and some salt and fry until reddish-brown, sprinkling in about a tablespoon of water to prevent burning.

2 Tie up the ground fennel seed and garam masala spices in a piece of muslin and add to the pan with the turmeric, ginger purée and yoghurt. Pour in 1 litre/1¾ pints water, cover and simmer on a very low heat for at least 2–3 hours. If the mixture becomes too dry, add a couple of tablespoons of water from time to time.

3 When the meat becomes soft and starts to stick to the fingers, add the turnips and sugar and cook for another 30 minutes.

4 At the end of cooking there should be only a little liquid left. Remove the muslin bag and garnish with the chopped coriander

Serves 4–6

200g/7oz ghee or clarified
   butter (see page 23)
¼ teaspoon asafoetida
4 cloves
1kg/2¼lb shoulder of lamb,
   cut into large cubes on the
   bone (ask your butcher to
   do this)
1 teaspoon red chilli powder
1 teaspoon ground fennel seed
1 teaspoon whole Garam
   Masala spices (see page 24),
   made to step 1
1½ teaspoons ground
   turmeric

2 tablespoons Ginger Purée
   (see page 22)
200g/7oz yoghurt, preferably
   Greek yoghurt, whisked
500g/1lb 2oz turnips, peeled
   and quartered
1 teaspoon sugar
a bunch of fresh coriander,
   chopped
salt to taste

Serve with *Gucchi Pulao* (see below). Fried onions, which are used to garnish this dish, are available ready cooked in supermarkets and Indian stores.

Khurmani Ka Murg

Chicken with apricots

1 Soak the dried apricots in hot water until softened. Heat the ghee or clarified butter in a large pan and add the yoghurt. Stir for 10 minutes, until the yoghurt turns brown, then add the apricots and cook, stirring, for 5 minutes.

2 Add the chicken pieces to the pan and cook, stirring, for 5 minutes, until lightly coloured. Add all the remaining ingredients except the flaked almonds, then pour in 400ml/14fl oz water and bring to the boil.

3 Simmer for 20 minutes, until the chicken is tender. Garnish with the flaked almonds.

Serves 4–6

100g/4oz dried apricots
50g/2oz ghee or clarified butter (see page 23)
100g/4oz yoghurt, preferably Greek yoghurt, whisked
8 chicken pieces, skinned (weighing about 1kg/2¼lb)
4 teaspoons ground fennel seed
2 teaspoons ground ginger
1 teaspoon ground cinnamon
½ teaspoon cumin seeds
4 green cardamom pods
½ teaspoon red chilli powder
4 tablespoons Fried Onion Purée (see page 23)
4 tablespoons blanched almonds, halved
1 tablespoon flaked almonds
fried onions
salt to taste

Gucchi Pulao

Mushroom pilaf

1 Strain the mushrom soaking water and reserve. Clean the morels thoroughly in cold running water, then drain.

2 Heat half the clarified butter or oil in a pan, add the morels and fry for 2–3 minutes. Add the salt and 200ml/7fl oz water and cook for another 5–7 minutes, until the morels are tender and have absorbed the water. Remove from the heat and set aside.

3 In a separate pan, heat the remaining clarified butter or oil and add the whole spices and bay leaf. Fry until they begin to splutter, then add the onion, ginger, chilli and yoghurt and fry until golden brown. Add the rice, the morel soaking liquid and 325ml/11fl oz water and bring to the boil. Reduce the heat to very low and cook, covered, for 20–25 minutes, until the rice is tender.

4 Mix the morels into the rice and continue cooking until there is no moisture left. Leave over a very low heat or on a hot plate for 5 minutes. Then garnish with the almonds, pistachios, cashew nuts and the lime zest and serve.

Serves 4–6

10g/¼oz dried morel mushrooms, soaked in 4 tablespoons of boiling water for 30 minutes, drained (water reserved) and cut in half lengthways
4 tablespoons clarified butter (see page 23) or vegetable oil
1 teaspoon salt
1 cinnamon stick
3 cloves
3 green cardamom pods
1 bay leaf
1 tablespoon very finely chopped onion
1 teaspoon very finely chopped fresh ginger
1 green chilli, cut in half
1 tablespoon yoghurt, preferably Greek yoghurt, whisked
250g/9oz basmati rice
1 tablespoon each almonds, pistachios and cashew nuts
finely chopped zest of 1 lime

When kidney beans are fully cooked, the skins will be cracked or peeling, not intact.

When pressed the beans must be soft.

Rajma

Spiced kidney beans

1 Drain the soaked beans, then put them in a pan and add double the volume of water. Add the turmeric, ground fennel seed, ginger, bay leaves and some salt, bring to the boil and boil hard for 10 minutes. Reduce the heat and simmer until the beans are tender.

2 Heat the ghee or oil in a separate pan. Add the asafoetida, cumin seeds, chilli powder and green chilli purée. Cook until they start to splutter, then add them to the beans.

3 Add the ground pomegranate seeds (or lemon juice) and garam masala and simmer for 5 minutes. Garnish with the fresh coriander leaves and strips of ginger before serving.

Serves 4–6

250g/9oz dried red kidney beans, soaked in cold water overnight

½ teaspoon ground turmeric

1 tablespoon ground fennel seed

½ tablespoon ground ginger

3 bay leaves

2 tablespoons ghee (see page 23) or vegetable oil

¼ teaspoon asafoetida

1 teaspoon cumin seeds

1 teaspoon red chilli powder

1 teaspoon Green Chilli Purée (see page 22)

1 teaspoon ground pomegranate seeds (or 1 tablespoon lemon juice)

1 teaspoon Garam Masala (see page 24)

20g/¾oz fresh coriander leaves

large knob of fresh ginger, cut into juliennne strips

salt to taste

Red kidney beans are best enjoyed when freshly picked from the plant; then they just need steaming and are simply irresistible. The more common dried version needs soaking.

There are a lot of variations on this famous dish. Vegetables such as okra,

jackfruit and colcasia can be cooked with the potatoes in the same manner.

Dum Aloo

Whole spiced potatoes

1 Peel the potatoes and prick them all over with a fork. In a deep pan, heat the mustard oil to smoking point, then deep-fry the potatoes in it until golden brown. Remove and set aside.

2 Heat a little of the same oil in a separate pan, add the cloves, cumin and asafoetida and fry until they start to splutter.

3 Add the potatoes, chilli powder, coriander, salt and 400ml/14fl oz water. Bring to the boil and simmer for 5 minutes, then stir in the ginger purée, shredded ginger and sugar and cook for a further 5 minutes.

4 Add the yoghurt and cook on a low heat for 10 minutes. Sprinkle with the garam masala and serve.

Serves 4–6

1kg/2¼lb baby new potatoes
250ml/8fl oz mustard oil
4 cloves
½ teaspoon cumin seeds
¼ teaspoon asafoetida
½ teaspoon red chilli powder
1 teaspoon ground coriander
1 teaspoon Ginger Purée (see page 24)
1 tablespoon finely shredded fresh ginger
1 teaspoon sugar
100g/4oz yoghurt, preferably Greek yoghurt, whisked
1 tablespoon Garam Masala (see page 24)
salt to taste

Karamkalla

Stir-fried spiced cabbage

Serves 4–6

100ml/3¹/2fl oz mustard oil
¹/4 teaspoon asafoetida
¹/2 teaspoon cumin seeds
a pinch of fenugreek seeds
1 teaspoon Ginger Purée (see page 22)
1 teaspoon finely chopped green chilli
¹/2 teaspoon ground ginger
1 large white or green cabbage (not Savoy), cut into 10cm/4 inch pieces
¹/2 teaspoon red chilli powder
a generous pinch of Garam Masala (see page 24)
1 teaspoon sugar
a pinch of ground turmeric
¹/2 teaspoon ground coriander
1 tablespoon chopped fresh coriander
salt to taste

1 In a large pan, heat the oil to smoking point, then add the asafoetida, cumin seeds, fenugreek seeds, ginger purée, green chilli and ground ginger.

2 Immediately add the cabbage, chilli powder, garam masala, sugar, turmeric, ground coriander and some salt and stir until well mixed.

3 Add 2 tablespoons of water and cook, uncovered, over a medium heat for about 15 minutes, until the cabbage is tender and there is no liquid left. Add the chopped coriander and toss well before serving.

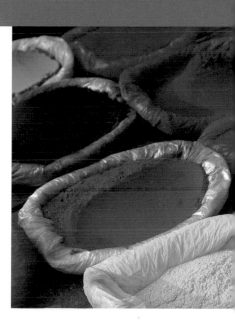

The Moghlai style of cooking was adopted by several maharajas and nawabs, most notably the rulers of Hyderabad, Awadh, Rampur and Patiala.

Moghlai

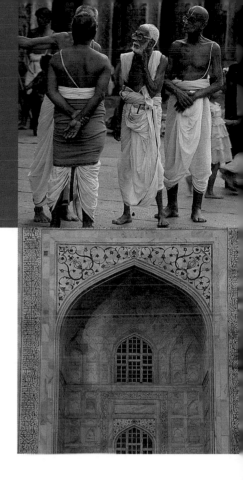

The Great Moghuls, probably history's grandest dynasty, were epicures. Moghul style blossomed in the 16th century, in the reign of the third emperor, Akbar, a period of great stability. Family life was based in the harem, where the emperor ate all his meals. The harem was a city in itself, with 5,000 members at its zenith, including princesses, amazonian guards and eunuchs. Vast quantities of exquisite food, dried and fresh fruit such as mangoes, melons, grapes, peaches, pomegranates, pineapple, and custard apple, brought from Kashmir, Kabul, Samarkand and Kandahar, were consumed. A contemporary European traveller wrote that Moghul ladies drank a great deal of expensive wine from Shiraz, a habit acquired from their husbands. Abul Fazal, the historian of Emperor Akbar's reign, wrote of the imperial kitchens: 'Cooks from all countries prepare a great variety of dishes of all kinds of grains, greens, meats; also oily, sweet and spicy dishes. The victuals are served in dishes of gold and silver, stone and earthenware. Some victuals are also kept half-ready so that in the space of an hour a hundred dishes are served up.' Despite these elaborate preparations, Akbar ate lightly and only once a day, abstained from eating meat on several days, including Fridays and in November, his birth month, and drank only pure Ganges water – he called it the 'water of immortality'.

Akbar's son, Jahangir, describes fantastic parties arranged for him by favourite queens. A single dinner, for example, hosted by Empress Noor Jahan in 1617 to celebrate a great military victory, cost her Rs.300,000, equivalent to about £3 million today. Incidentally, Jahangir's son, Emperor Shahjahan, built the wondrous Taj Mahal.

Scholars argue that the nomadic and barbaric Moghuls, descendants of Mongols, could not have created a distinctive cuisine before they settled in India. Moghul emperors, however, took what they found in India, notably the food of the Hindu kayast kitchens, added nuts, saffron and cream to create fusion cuisine now called Moghlai. Tomatoes, brought to India by the Portuguese, were first used by Empress Noor Jahan with browned onions to create the moghul curry sauce. The anglicised word 'curry', derived from the Tamil word *kari* or sauce, describes an aromatized stew simmered in water in a heavy pan over gentle heat that helps to blend the flavours.

The internationally popular Moghlai food today is a lighter version of food made for the emperors, substituting oil for ghee and using less cream and nuts.

A very effective soup for helping the system to fight cold, and strengthen your bones. It provides energy and keeps you warm in winter.

Murg Shorba

Chicken and yoghurt soup

Serves 4–6

1kg/2¼lb raw chicken bones
6 tablespoons vegetable oil
150g/5oz red onions, finely
    chopped
250g/9oz tomatoes, finely
    chopped
250g/9oz yoghurt, preferably
    Greek yoghurt, whisked
3 green chillies (left whole)
2 tablespoons crushed garlic
1 tablespoon finely chopped
    fresh ginger
1 tablespoon chopped fresh
    mint
2 teaspoons ground coriander
1 teaspoon Garam Masala
    (see page 24)
½ teaspoon ground turmeric
1 teaspoon red chilli powder
1 teaspoon cumin seeds,
    roasted in a dry frying pan
    and then ground
2 teaspoons finely chopped
    fresh coriander
julienne strips of tomato
shredded cooked chicken, to
    garnish (optional)
salt to taste

For tempering:

2 teaspoons vegetable oil
1 teaspoon cumin seeds
¼ teaspoon onion seeds
    (nigella seeds)
2 tablespoons gram flour
    (chickpea flour)

1 Bring 2 litres/3½ pints water to the boil in a large pan, add the chicken bones and blanch for 1 minute. Drain and set aside.

2 Heat the oil in a pan, add the onions and fry until golden brown. Add all the remaining ingredients except the chicken bones and fresh coriander and stir-fry for 30 seconds.

3 Add the chicken bones and stir-fry for 5 minutes. Then add 4 litres/7 pints water and bring to the boil, skimming off the scum from the surface. Reduce the heat to as low as possible and simmer gently for 45 minutes. Strain the stock through a muslin cloth into a clean pan and bring back to a simmer.

4 Heat the oil for tempering in a small pan, add the cumin and onion seeds and fry until they start to splutter. Add the gram flour and fry till it turns golden brown. Add this mixture to the chicken stock and simmer for 10 minutes. Garnish with the chopped fresh coriander, cooked chicken strips, if using, and julienne of tomato.

Home-made soups are rarely thick in India. The emphasis is on flavours to rejuvenate the tastebuds, and induce the appetite.

Murg Tikka Masala has always been popular in India, but as a dry dish.

A popular variation is made with added fresh cream to provide the sauce.

Murg Tikka Masala

Chicken tikka masala

Serves 4–6

1kg/2¼lb boneless chicken
  breasts, cut into bite-sized
  pieces

For the marinade:

½ teaspoon Ginger Purée (see
  page 22)
½ teaspoon Garlic Purée (see
  page 22)
1½ teaspoons lemon juice
1 tablespoon vegetable oil
100g/4oz yoghurt, preferably
  Greek yoghurt, whisked
1 teaspoon cumin seeds,
  roasted in a dry frying pan
  and then ground
½ teaspoon red chilli powder
salt to taste

For the sauce:

150ml/¼ pint vegetable oil
625g/1lb 6oz Raw Onion
  Purée (see page 22)
1 teaspoon Ginger Purée (see
  page 22)
1 teaspoon Garlic Purée (see
  page 22)
1 teaspoon Green Chilli Purée
  (see page 22)
1 teaspoon red chilli powder
½ teaspoon ground turmeric
1 teaspoon ground coriander
300g/11oz fresh tomatoes,
  puréed
3 tablespoons single cream
2 tablespoons chopped fresh
  coriander
¼ teaspoon Garam Masala
  (see page 24)
salt to taste

1 Mix together all the ingredients for the marinade. Add the chicken, making sure it is well coated, and leave to marinate for 2 hours.

2 Spread the chicken pieces out on a baking tray and cook in an oven preheated to 180°C/350°F/Gas Mark 4 for 15 minutes (ideally it should be cooked in a tandoor, which is how it is done traditionally).

3 For the sauce, heat the oil in a pan, add the onion purée and cook, stirring, until it is golden brown. Add the ginger, garlic and green chilli purées and stir-fry for 2 minutes. Add the ground spices and stir-fry for 30 seconds. Add 250ml/8fl oz water and the puréed tomatoes and cook for 12–15 minutes, until the mixture has the consistency of double cream.

4 Add the chicken pieces to the sauce and cook for 5–8 minutes. Stir in the cream and chopped coriander, then sprinkle over the garam masala.

Marinate and cook the chicken as for *Murg Tikka Masala*

(opposite) but serve with the following sauces:

Murg Mumtaz

Chicken in tomato, fenugreek and almond gravy

1 Prepare the chicken as on page 42 to the end of step 2. For the sauce, put the puréed tomatoes, ginger, garlic and green chilli purées and ground spices in a pan with 500ml/17fl oz water and bring to the boil. Simmer for 30 minutes, then strain through a sieve into a clean pan. Simmer for 10 minutes.

2 Put the toasted flaked almonds in a blender with 300ml/ ½ pint water and blend to a smooth paste. Add to the pan with all the remaining ingredients and the chicken tikka and simmer for 10 minutes.

Serves 4–6

chicken and marinade as for Chicken Tikka Masala (see page 42)
1kg/2¼lb fresh tomatoes, puréed
½ teaspoon Ginger Purée (see page 22)
1 teaspoon Garlic Purée (see page 22)
½ teaspoon Green Chilli Purée (see page 22)
1 teaspoon red chilli powder
½ teaspoon ground cloves
1 teaspoon ground green cardamom
200g/7oz toasted flaked almonds
200g/7oz butter
150ml/¼ pint single cream
2 teaspoons ground fenugreek leaves
1 teaspoon Garam Masala (see page 24)
salt to taste

Murg Makhani

Butter chicken

1 Prepare the chicken as on page 42 to the end of step 2. For the sauce, put the puréed tomatoes, ginger, garlic and green chilli purées, chilli powder, crushed peppercorns, coriander stalks, bay leaves, cloves and cardamom in a pan with 500ml/17fl oz water and salt to taste. Bring to the boil and simmer for 30 minutes.

2 Strain the mixture through a fine sieve into a clean pan and simmer for 10 minutes. Add all the remaining ingredients and the chicken tikka and simmer for a further 10 minutes, until the sauce is the consistency of double cream.

Serves 4–6

chicken and marinade as for Chicken Tikka Masala (see page 42)
1kg/2¼lb fresh tomatoes, puréed
1 teaspoon Ginger Purée (see page 22)
1 teaspoon Garlic Purée (see page 22)
½ teaspoon Green Chilli Purée (see page 22)
½ teaspoon red chilli powder
½ teaspoon black peppercorns, crushed
2 teaspoons chopped fresh coriander stalks
2–3 bay leaves
a pinch of ground cloves
½ teaspoon ground green cardamom
75g/3oz butter
100ml/3½fl oz single cream
½ teaspoon ground fenugreek
a pinch of Garam Masala (see page 24)
1 tablespoon sugar
salt to taste

Moghlai dishes are all derived from the royal kitchens of the Moghuls. The rich and delicate flavours are a revelation.

Traditionally, meat was beaten with spices and fat into smaller pieces

on a stone slab to keep the meat cold and ensure tenderness.

Badami Kofta

Lamb meatballs with almonds

1 For the meatballs, mix everything together except the almonds (but including the ice, which keeps the meatballs well chilled) and mince to a very fine paste. Keep in the fridge.

2 For the sauce, put the toasted almonds in a blender with 100ml/3½fl oz water and blend to a paste.

3 Heat the ghee or clarified butter in a pan, add the whole spices and fry until they begin to splutter. Add the puréed onions and cook, stirring, until they turn golden brown. Then add the puréed tomatoes, turmeric, chilli powder, garlic, ginger and green chilli purées and some salt and cook, stirring, for about 15 minutes, until the oil separates from the mixture.

4 Add 500ml/17fl oz water, the almond paste and the sugar and simmer for 30 minutes. Meanwhile, take the meat mixture out of the fridge and shape into 24 balls. Stuff each ball with a blanched almond, reshaping if necessary so the almond is completely enclosed.

5 Put the meatballs into the sauce and poach on a very low heat for 20 minutes. Drizzle over the cream and chopped coriander.

Serves 4–6

600g/1lb 5oz boneless shoulder of lamb, cut into 2.5cm/1 inch cubes
50g/2oz lamb fat
2 eggs
1 teaspoon ground black cardamom
1½ teaspoons ground green cardamom
½ teaspoon ground cloves
1 teaspoon ground cinnamon
1 tablespoon finely chopped fresh ginger
1 tablespoon chopped fresh coriander stalks
50g/2oz ice, crushed
24 blanched almonds
salt to taste

For the sauce:

50g/2oz toasted flaked almonds
100g/4oz ghee or clarified butter (see page 23)
4 green cardamom pods
2 black cardamom pods
2 cinnamon sticks
200g/7oz onions, puréed
150g/5oz fresh tomatoes, puréed
¼ teaspoon ground turmeric
1 teaspoon red chilli powder
1 tablespoon Garlic Purée (see page 22)
1 teaspoon Ginger Purée (see page 22)
1 teaspoon Green Chilli Purée (see page 22)
1 tablespoon sugar
4 tablespoons single cream
1 tablespoon chopped fresh coriander
salt to taste

Moghlai cooks were very creative, and the inclusions of cream, yogurt and fruits with vegetables are attributed to their expertise.

Tarkari Biryani

Mixed vegetable and cheese biryani

1 Soak the rice in cold water for 1 hour, then drain and parboil in 3 litres/5 pints salted water for 8–10 minutes. Drain off excess water and set aside. Warm the milk, add the saffron and rosewater and set aside for 30 minutes.

2 Heat the ghee or clarified butter in a pan, add the whole spices and fry until they begin to splutter. Add the vegetables, paneer, cashew nuts, raisins and green chilli and stir-fry for 5 minutes.

3 Add the cream and some salt and bring to the boil. Simmer for 5 minutes and then remove from the heat (this is the vegetable curry for the biryani).

4 Layer the rice and vegetable curry in a greased ovenproof dish, sprinkling each layer of vegetable curry with the ground cardamom, mace and ground fenugreek leaves. There should be at least 3 layers of rice with 2 layers of curry. Pour the saffron mixture over the top.

5 Cover tightly with foil and cook for 1 hour in an oven preheated to 150°C/300°F/Gas Mark 2.

Serves 4–6

600g/1lb 5oz basmati rice
100ml/3½fl oz milk
4 pinches of saffron
2 tablespoons rosewater
200g/7oz ghee or clarified butter (see page 23)
6 green cardamom pods
2 cinnamon sticks
3 bay leaves
5 cloves
2 blades of mace
100g/4oz cauliflower florets
100g/4oz peas
100g/4oz potatoes, peeled and cut into 1cm/½ inch cubes
100g/4oz carrots, peeled and cut into 1cm/½ inch cubes
100g/4oz button mushrooms, quartered
100g/4oz paneer, cut into 1cm/½ inch cubes
50g/2oz cashew nuts
50g/2oz raisins
1 tablespoon finely chopped green chilli
750ml/1¼ pints single cream
25g/1oz ground green cardamom
½ teaspoon ground mace
2 teaspoons ground fenugreek leaves
salt to taste

Dum is a method of cooking outdoors – to cook the results of a day's hunting –

in stoves dug underground to protect the wood fires from the wind.

Dum Ka Murg

Chicken in onion, yoghurt and almond gravy

Serves 4–6

3 tablespoons ghee or clarified
  butter (see page 23)
250g/9oz onions, sliced
50g/2oz toasted flaked
  almonds
1 teaspoon ground coriander
a pinch of ground turmeric
½ teaspoon Garlic Purée (see
  page 22)
250g/9oz yoghurt, preferably
  Greek yoghurt, whisked

a pinch of Garam Masala (see
  page 24)
1kg/2¼lb boneless chicken
  breasts, cut into bite-sized
  pieces
1 teaspoon tomato purée
toasted cashew nuts
zest of 1 lime
salt to taste

1 Heat the ghee or clarified butter in a pan, add the onions and sauté until golden brown. Remove the onions from the pan with a slotted spoon, drain on kitchen paper and purée in a blender with 100ml/3½fl oz water. Set aside.

2 Put the toasted flaked almonds in a blender with 200ml/7fl oz water and whizz to a paste, then set aside.

3 Reheat the ghee in which the onions were cooked, add the coriander, turmeric, garlic purée, yoghurt, garam masala, some salt and 400ml/14fl oz water. Cook, stirring, for 5 minutes, until the mixture acquires a sandy texture.

4 Add the chicken and cook, stirring, for 5 minutes. Finally add the onion and almond purées and the tomato purée and simmer for 10 minutes, until the sauce has a coating consistency. Garnish with the cashew nuts and lime zest and serve.

Moghuls loved hunting wildfowl and incorporated several

aromatic spices in their recipes for cooking it.

Achari Bateyr

Spiced whole quail

Serves 4–6

4 tablespoons mustard oil

¾ teaspoon whole Achari
   Spice Mix (see page 24)

250g/9oz onions, chopped

300g/11oz tomatoes, finely
   chopped

¾ teaspoon ground Achari
   Spice Mix (see page 24)

1 teaspoon ground coriander

1 teaspoon ground cumin

1 teaspoon red chilli powder

⅓ teaspoon ground turmeric

1 teaspoon dried mango
   powder

½ teaspoon ground fenugreek
   leaves

½ teaspoon Ginger Purée (see
   page 22)

1 teaspoon Garlic Purée (see
   page 22)

4 quails

1 tablespoon lemon juice

1 teaspoon finely chopped
   fresh coriander

salt to taste

1 Heat the mustard oil in a large pan, add the whole achari
spices and fry until they begin to splutter. Add the onions and
stir-fry until they turn golden brown.

2 Add the tomatoes, all the ground spices, the ginger and garlic
purées and some salt and cook, stirring, for 15 minutes. Add the
quails and fry until browned all over.

3 Cover the pan and cook on a very low heat for 15 minutes or
until the quails are tender. Stir in the lemon juice and fresh
coriander. Serve with naan bread.

Venison was the favourite meat of the Moghuls – it was purported to possess aphrodisiac qualities! Serve the venison on a bed of *Saag Paneer* (see below).

Janglee Maans

Venison in spicy sauce

1 Heat the ghee or clarified butter in a pan, add the whole spices and cook until they begin to splutter. Add the onions and stir-fry until they turn golden brown.

2 Add the venison, the ginger and garlic purées, chilli powder, turmeric, coriander, yoghurt and some salt and cook, stirring, over a medium heat for 20 minutes. Add 150ml/¼ pint water and cook for 20 minutes, stirring occasionally.

3 Add 250ml/8fl oz water, then cover and cook on a very low heat for 25 minutes, until the meat is tender. Stir in the garam masala.

Serves 4–6

150g/5oz ghee or clarified
   butter (see page 23)
5–6 dried red chillies
6–8 green cardamom pods
3–4 black cardamom pods
6–8 cloves
200g/7oz onions, finely
   chopped
1kg/2¼lb boneless venison,
   cut into 2.5cm/1 inch cubes
1 tablespoon Ginger Purée
   (see page 22)
2 tablespoons Garlic Purée
   (see page 22)
1 tablespoon red chilli powder
½ teaspoon ground turmeric
1 tablespoon ground
   coriander
150g/5oz yoghurt, preferably
   Greek yoghurt, whisked
1 teaspoon Garam Masala
   (see page 24)
salt to taste

Saag Paneer

Spinach and cheese

Serves 4–6

2kg/4½lb fresh spinach, well
   washed
50g/2oz ghee or clarified
   butter (see page 23)
½ teaspoon cumin seeds
50g/2oz onions, finely
   chopped
50g/2oz tomatoes, finely
   chopped
1 teaspoon Garlic Purée (see
   page 22)
1 tablespoon finely chopped
   fresh ginger
½ teaspoon red chilli powder
½ teaspoon ground coriander
200g/7oz paneer, cut into
   1cm/½ inch dice
2 tablespoons single cream
1 teaspoon lemon juice
2 teaspoon chopped fresh
   coriander
salt to taste

1 Bring a large pan of water to the boil and briefly blanch the spinach leaves. Drain well and refresh in cold water to retain their bright green colour. Drain again and then purée, or chop finely, the spinach in a blender.

2 Heat the ghee or clarified butter in a pan, add the cumin seeds and fry until they begin to splutter. Add the chopped onions and stir-fry until they turn golden brown. Then add the tomatoes, garlic purée, chopped ginger, chilli powder, ground coriander and some salt and stir-fry for 2 minutes.

3 Add the paneer cubes and stir-fry for 30 seconds. Then add the spinach purée and cook for 3-4 minutes. Stir in the cream, lemon juice and chopped coriander.

Only the elite could afford to hunt. Once caught, the venison was cooked and consumed in the jungle, using just a few other ingredients carried by the hunters on their trek.

This is a definitive festive celebration dish, with infinite methods of preparation;

all over India people have their own ways of making *biryani*.

Lamb Biryani

Lamb with fragrant basmati rice

1 Heat the ghee or clarified butter in a large pan, add the whole spices and fry for 10 seconds. Add the lamb and sauté until lightly browned.

2 Add the yoghurt, chilli powder, ginger purée and asafoetida and cook over a low heat for about 1 hour, until the meat is tender. Stir every 5 minutes to prevent the mixture sticking. The liquid (the juices from the meat) should become a coating consistency.

3 Stir in all the remaining spices and cook for 5 minutes. Add 200ml/7 fl oz water, bring to the boil, simer for 5 minutes and remove from the heat.

4 Parboil the rice with a pinch of salt in 1.5 litres/2½ pints water for 8–10 minutes. Drain off the excess water and set aside.

5 Warm the milk and add the saffron to it. In a greased ovenproof dish, sprinkle half the rice, then half the rosewater, saffron milk and lamb. Repeat with the remaining ingredients. Cover the dish with foil and bake for 1 hour in an oven preheated to 150°C/300°F/Gas Mark 2.

Serves 4–6

150g/5oz ghee or clarified butter (see page 23)
2 cinnamon sticks
6 green cardamom pods
6 cloves
600g/1lb 5oz boneless leg of lamb, cut into 2.5cm/1 inch cubes
200g/7oz yoghurt, preferably Greek yoghurt, whisked
1 teaspoon red chilli powder
2 teaspoons Ginger Purée (see page 22)
a pinch of asafoetida
½ teaspoon ground cumin
a pinch of ground cloves
½ teaspoon ground green cardamom
300g/11oz basmati rice
200ml/7fl oz milk
2 pinches of saffron
4 teaspoons rosewater
salt to taste

A kadhai is a wok, generally an iron one. Food cooked

in a kadhai has a distinctive roasted, smoky flavour.

Kadhai Chholey

Chickpeas with tomatoes and chilli

1 Drain the chickpeas and put them in a pan with 2 litres/ 3½ pints water, the bicarbonate of soda and some salt. Boil until tender, then drain off excess liquid and set aside.

2 Heat the ghee or clarified butter in a pan, add the cumin seeds and cook until they start to crackle. Add the onions and sauté until golden brown, then add the garlic purée and cook, stirring, for 30 seconds. Add the chopped tomatoes, tomato purée, chillies, chholey masala and some salt and stir-fry for 2 minutes.

3 Add the boiled chickpeas and 200ml/7fl oz water and cook until all the water has been absorbed. Stir in the lemon juice and shredded ginger.

Serves 4–6

250g/9oz chickpeas, soaked in
  cold water overnight
¼ teaspoon bicarbonate of
  soda
75g/3oz ghee or clarified
  butter (see page 23)
1 teaspoon cumin seeds
400g/14oz onions, chopped
25g/1oz Garlic Purée (see
  page 22)
600g/1lb 5oz tomatoes,
  chopped
1 tablespoon tomato purée
4 green chillies, chopped
25g/1oz Chholey Masala (see
  page 25)
2 tablespoons lemon juice
40g/1½oz fresh ginger, finely
  shredded
salt to taste

One of the earliest tandoori restaurants in Delhi was Moti Mahal, owned by refugees fleeing to the city when the country was partitioned in 1947.

Tandoor

Delhi was the capital of kings for a thousand years and the silhouette of seven ancient cities line the sky, amongst them the ruins of the Old Fort, Tughlaqabad and the Red Fort built by the Moghul Emperor Shahjahan. The last historic city to be built was New Delhi, designed by the British architect Lutyens when the capital of the Raj was shifted to Delhi from Calcutta in 1911. It's ironic that, despite the fact that the British first arrived in India to search for spices, food at the height of the Raj was made as bland and as much like English food as possible. East Indiamen came for pepper that was needed in Europe to preserve meat and mull wine. Salt was always important – the word salary derives from it because in ancient times Roman soldiers were paid partly in salt – but in the hot Indian climate it is vital and Mahatma Gandhi understood this when he led the famous Salt March that helped to end the Raj.

Meanwhile, after a thousand years of Hindu, Muslim, Sikh and British influence, Delhi became a unique city in its architecture, food and culture, but one of the most popular foods with all communities proved to be Tandoori cuisine.

The tandoor, an open clay oven, is an ancient Indian invention. Its circumference is designed to spread heat evenly and tandoori bread is believed to have been made in India for over 5,000 years. There are many variations of tandoori bread: *naan* is made with self-raising flour kneaded with yogurt and milk; the flaky, layered *parantha* is wholemeal flour kneaded with oil or ghee, and a tandoori *roti* is a lighter version of the tandoori *parantha*, minus the oil/ghee.

There are three types of tandoors – the small domestic tandoor made of clay and iron; the much larger commercial tandoor with brick walls that are cemented; and the biggest of all, the commercial iron tandoor used to bake rich butter *rotis* and other delicacies. The mouth of the tandoor should be near the cook and the opening at the bottom facing away from him so that he does not feel the heat. Coal or coke is the preferred medium for tandoori cooking to provide a slow, medium heat.

It was only when the use of meat tenderizers, such as papaya, was properly understood that meat began to be cooked in the tandoor. Marination is very important in tandoori cooking and the most widely used tenderisers are kachri pod, raw papaya and yogurt. All three are often used when cooking *raan mussalam*, for example, since it's a whole leg of lamb and, if well marinated, it melts in the mouth.

Malai Kebab

Chicken kebabs

1 Mix the chicken with all the ingredients for the first marinade and set aside for 30 minutes.

2 Mix together all the ingredients for the second marinade to form a thick paste and season with salt. Add the chicken pieces, mix well and set aside for 2 hours.

3 Put the chicken pieces on skewers and cook in an oven preheated to 180°C/350°F/Gas Mark 4 for 15 minutes, or in a moderately hot tandoor oven for 6–8 minutes. Baste with the oil and cook for another 2–3 minutes.

4 Squeeze the lemon juice on to the chicken and then sprinkle over the chat masala. Serve with the onion, tomato and lettuce, if liked.

Serves 4–6

1kg/2¼lb boneless chicken
breasts, cut into bite-sized
pieces
100ml/3½fl oz vegetable oil

For the first
marinade:

4 tablespoons lemon juice
1 teaspoon Ginger Purée (see
page 22)
1 teaspoon Garlic Purée (see
page 22)
salt to taste

For the second
marinade:

150g/5oz cream cheese
400ml/14fl oz single cream
a pinch of ground nutmeg
a pinch of ground mace
½ teaspoon ground green
cardamom
½ teaspoon ground white
pepper
1 teaspoon finely chopped
green chilli
2 tablespoons finely chopped
fresh coriander
1 teaspoon finely chopped
fresh ginger

To serve:

½ teaspoon lemon juice
¼ teaspoon Chat Masala (see
page 23)
1 onion, very thinly sliced
1 tomato, sliced
2 lettuce leaves, shredded

Sole or pomfret could be substituted for the trout.

A small salad of onion, tomato and lettuce can be served with the fish.

Tandoori Machhi

Tandoori trout

Serves 4–6

4 x 250g/9oz trout, cleaned
150ml/¼ pint vegetable oil

For the first marinade:

4 tablespoons lemon juice
1 teaspoon Ginger Purée (see page 22)
1 teaspoon Garlic Purée (see page 22)
salt to taste

For the second marinade:

4 teaspoons gram flour (chickpea flour), fried in 4 teaspoons ghee until it turns a very pale brown
4 tablespoons vegetable oil
1 teaspoon Ginger Purée (see page 22)
1 teaspoon Garlic Purée (see page 22)
350g/12oz yoghurt, preferably Greek yoghurt, whisked

225g/8oz fresh coriander, coarsely chopped
100g/4oz mint, coarsely chopped
4 green chillies, chopped
4 garlic cloves, chopped
4cm/1½ inch piece of fresh ginger, chopped
2 teaspoons dried mango powder
½ teaspoon cumin seeds, roasted in a dry frying pan and then ground

To serve:

2 tablespoons lemon juice
½ teaspoon Chat Masala (see page 23)

1 Make 3–4 deep cuts on each side of the trout. Mix together all the ingredients for the first marinade, rub over the trout and set aside for 30 minutes.

2 Put all the ingredients for the second marinade in a blender, add some salt and process until smooth. Spread the marinade over the trout and set aside for 2 hours.

3 Put the fish on a rack over a baking tray and cook in an oven preheated to 180°C/350°F/Gas Mark 4 for 20 minutes, or in a moderately hot tandoor for 10–12 minutes. Baste with the vegetable oil and then cook for a further 2–3 minutes.

4 Sprinkle the lemon juice and chat masala over the trout and serve.

Carom seeds, also known as lovage,

take the delicious salmon to new taste horizons.

Salmon Ka Tikka

Marinated salmon

Serves 4–6
1kg/2¼lb salmon fillet, skinned and cut into bite-sized pieces
100ml/3½ fl oz vegetable oil

For the first marinade:
150ml/¼ pint lemon juice
1 teaspoon Ginger Purée (see page 22)
1 teaspoon Garlic Purée (see page 22)
salt to taste

For the second marinade:
2 tablespoons chopped fresh dill
400ml/14fl oz single cream
1 tablespoon honey
¼ teaspoon carom seeds
1½ teaspoons English mustard
150g/5oz cream cheese
1 teaspoon ground green cardamom
½ teaspoon crushed black peppercorns

To serve:
2 tablespoons lemon juice
½ teaspoon Chat Masala (see page 23)
1 onion, very thinly sliced
1 tomato, sliced
2 lettuce leaves, shredded

1 Mix together all the ingredients for the first marinade, add the salmon pieces and mix well. Set aside for 30 minutes.

2 Mix all the ingredients for the second marinade to a smooth paste, adding salt to taste, and mix with the fish. Set aside for 2 hours.

3 Put the salmon pieces on skewers and cook in an oven preheated to 180°C/350°F/Gas Mark 4 for 10 minutes, or in a moderately hot tandoor for 4–5 minutes. Baste with the vegetable oil and cook for a further minute or two.

4 Sprinkle the lemon juice and chat masala over the salmon and serve with the onion, tomato and lettuce.

Yoghurt is a natural tenderiser and, in dishes like this,

keeps the meat juicy and succulent, ensuring that the cooking time is as brief as possible.

Tandoori Murg

Tandoori chicken

Serves 4–6

650g/1lb 7oz whole skinned chicken, jointed into 4 pieces (a chicken this size is ideal for cooking in a tandoor oven but in a conventional oven you could use a bigger bird)
3 tablespoons vegetable oil

For the first marinade:

4 tablespoons lemon juice
¼ teaspoon red chilli powder
15g/½oz Ginger Purée (see page 22)
25g/1oz Garlic Purée (see page 22)
salt to taste

For the second marinade:

250g/9oz yoghurt, preferably Greek yoghurt, whisked
1 teaspoon lemon juice
5 tablespoons vegetable oil
¼ teaspoon red chilli powder
a pinch of Garam Masala (see page 24)

½ teaspoon cumin seeds, roasted in a dry frying pan and then ground
a pinch of ground fenugreek leaves
a pinch of ground green cardamom

To serve:

½ teaspoon lemon juice
¼ teaspoon Chat Masala (see page 23)
1 red onion, very thinly sliced in rings
lemon wedges

1 With a sharp knife, make 3 deep parallel cuts on each chicken breast, 2 parallel cuts on each thigh and 3 on each leg.

2 Mix together all the ingredients for the first marinade to a paste and rub it all over the chicken. Set aside for 30 minutes.

3 Mix together all the ingredients for the second marinade, adding salt to taste, and use to coat the chicken. Set aside for 2 hours.

4 Put the chicken pieces on a baking tray and cook in an oven preheated to 180°C/350°F/Gas Mark 4 for 25–30 minutes – or in a moderately hot tandoor oven for 12–15 minutes. Baste the chicken with the vegetable oil and cook for a further 2–3 minutes.

5 Squeeze the lemon juice on to the chicken and then sprinkle over the chat masala. Serve with the onion rings and lemon wedges.

Variation: Chicken Tikka

This is the same as tandoori chicken but uses boneless meat. Cut the chicken into bite-sized pieces, then marinate it as described, left. Reduce the cooking time to 15 minutes if using a conventional oven and 6–8 minutes if using a tandoor.

The *raan* can be served with gravy made with the leftover juices in the pan. Just add water, stir and cook for a few minutes.

Raan Mussalam

Roast lamb

Serves 4–6

1 leg of spring lamb, weighing about 800g/1¾lb

For the first marinade:

2 tablespoons malt vinegar

1 tablespoon red chilli powder

1 tablespoon Ginger Purée (see page 22)

1½ tablespoons Garlic Purée (see page 22)

5 tablespoons vegetable oil

salt to taste

For the second marinade:

200g/7oz yoghurt, preferably Greek yoghurt, whisked

½ teaspoon ground cumin

½ teaspoon ground coriander

½ teaspoon Garam Masala (see page 24)

1 tablespoon paprika

¼ teaspoon ground black cardamom

¼ teaspoon ground green cardamom

a pinch of ground nutmeg

a pinch of ground cloves

1 bay leaf

1 teaspoon rosewater

¼ teaspoon ground cinnamon

To serve:

2 tablespoons lemon juice

½ teaspoon Chat Masala (see page 23)

1 spring onion, cut lengthways into thin shreds

1 Prick the leg of lamb all over with a fork. Mix together all the ingredients for the first marinade, spread over the meat and set aside for 2 hours.

2 Mix all the ingredients for the second marinade to a smooth paste, season with salt and spread the mixture all over the lamb. Put it in a roasting tin, cover with foil and cook in an oven preheated to 150°C/300°F/Gas Mark 2 for 3 hours.

3 Remove the meat from the oven, take it off the bone and cut it into bite-sized pieces. Pour the lemon juice on it, sprinkle with the chat masala and mix well. Arrange on a serving platter and decorate with the spring onion shreds.

Although the meat is taken off the bone after roasting,
traditionally the lamb bone is served on the plate.

Subz Kebab can be made from any combination of vegetables – except root vegetables such as potatoes, which can be skewered pre-cooked and then marinated.

Subz Kebab

Vegetable shashlik

1 Mix together all the ingredients for the marinade. Pour the marinade over the vegetables and paneer, if using, and set aside for 30 minutes. Soak some wooden skewers in cold water for 30 minutes.

2 Put the vegetables, and paneer if using, on the skewers and cook in an oven preheated to 180°C/350°F/Gas Mark 4 for 20 minutes or in a moderately hot tandoor for 10 minutes. Baste with the vegetable oil and cook for a further 2–3 minutes.

3 Sprinkle the vegetables with the lemon juice and chat masala.

Serves 4–6

200g/7oz red peppers, cut into 2.5cm/1 inch squares
200g/7oz green peppers, cut into 2.5cm/1 inch squares
200g/7oz yellow peppers, cut into 2.5cm/1 inch squares
200g/7oz button mushrooms, left whole
200g/7oz baby aubergines, cut in half
200g/7oz tomatoes, cut into 2.5cm/1 inch cubes
200g/7oz onions, cut into 2.5cm/1 inch squares
200g/7oz courgettes, cut into 2.5cm/1 inch cubes
200g/7oz paneer, cut into 2.5cm/1 inch cubes (optional)
2 tablespoons vegetable oil

For the marinade:

8 tablespoons yoghurt, preferably Greek yoghurt, whisked
1 teaspoon Ginger Purée (see page 22)
2 teaspoons Garlic Purée (see page 22)
4 teaspoons lemon juice
3 tablespoons vegetable oil

1 teaspoon Garam Masala (see page 24)
1 teaspoon ground pomegranate seeds
1 teaspoon crushed black peppercorns
1 teaspoon ground green cardamom
1 teaspoon ground anise seeds
1 teaspoon dry mango powder
2 teaspoons ground coriander
1 teaspoon ground cumin
1 teaspoon red chilli powder
1$\frac{1}{2}$ teaspoons Chat Masala (see page 23)
salt to taste

To serve:

2 tablespoons lemon juice
$\frac{1}{2}$ teaspoon Chat Masala (see page 23)

Traditional Indians, including Bengalis, eat with their fingers
and always with the right hand which is considered pure,
unlike the left hand that is used for ablutions.

Bengal

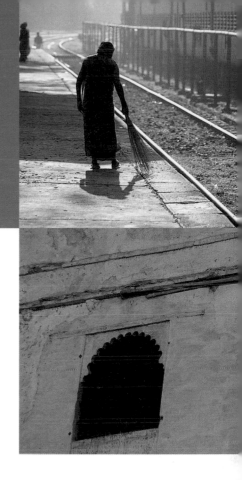

In Bengal, they consider fish to be a vegetarian dish, jokingly referred to either as *jal tori* (water gourd) or as the Fruit of the Ocean. Even Bengali Brahmins eat fish, although Brahmins are normally vegetarian. With numerous ponds, rivers and the teeming waters of the Bay of Bengal, it is no wonder that the people are enthusiastic fishetarians. However, a wide variety of vegetables also grow in the hot and humid climate, including the popular bananas that are eaten ripe, raw and cooked.

Bengal was linked to the rest of the world by trade from ancient times, especially with Armenia, Persia, Greece and China. Almost a hundred years before the British arrived, the Portuguese built a church and a township there. In 1690, Joe Charnock of the East India Company arrived at the mouth of the River Hooghly, at Kalighat, a place named after its presiding deity, the Goddess Kali. Later, East Indiamen created Calcutta (now called Kolkatta) and it became the capital of the British Raj. It is said that the first meal Charnock was offered by local villagers was *khitchuri*, a dish of rice and lentils. That evolved into kedgeree, a favoured dish of the Raj.

A typical Bengali meal would start with a bitter dish made with bitter gourd, neem leaves and green bananas, cooked in spices, followed by rice, daal and fish dishes. The most popular is the river fish Hilsa, a type of herring, typically fried in hot mustard oil with mustard and poppy seeds – mustard is to Bengal what coconut is to Goa, and mustard oil is used for frying while mustard seeds are used in cooking. Fish eyes and heads are considered to be delicacies, but, by convention, fish is not eaten at certain times of year that coincide with their breeding cycles.

The plentiful rice of Bengal is not the basmati of North India. Instead, there are other varieties such as Gopal and Kamini. A lot of Bengali rice is parboiled – a healthy method because the paddy retains the vitamins and nutrients contained in the husk. Cooking perfect rice was the test of a good cook in Bengal and a new daughter-in-law could curry favour with her in-laws if she could do that successfully.

The other distinct taste of Bengal is a sweet one. Milk-based sweets such as *rasmalai*, *rabri*, *rosogolla*, *sondesh*, and *chenna* are now popular all over India. In Bengali homes the meal could end with *mishti doi*, curd sweetened with dates, and a plate of dry sweets. Finally, a *paan*, betel-leaf, would put a full-stop to the meal, acting both as a digestive and mouth freshener.

Traditionally, the smallest prawns with their shells on, for a crunchy effect, would be used in this dish. Here we have peeled them.

Jheenga Charchari
Stir-fried prawns

1 Grind together the cumin, poppy and mustard seeds, turmeric, red chillies, onion, ginger and garlic.

2 In a small pan, heat the mustard oil to smoking point. Add all the tempering spices and let them splutter until the dried chillies change colour.

3 Add the ground spice mixture and stir-fry for 1 minute. Then add the prawns and stir-fry over a high heat for 2 minutes. Stir in the sugar and some salt and cook for about a minute longer, until the oil separates from the mixture.

Serves 4–6

1 teaspoon cumin seeds
1 teaspoon poppy seeds
1 teaspoon mustard seeds
1 teaspoon ground turmeric
4 dried red chillies
1 large onion, chopped
1cm/^{1}/$_2$ inch piece of fresh
   ginger, chopped
5 garlic cloves, chopped
1kg/2^1/$_4$lb medium-sized raw
   headless prawns, shelled
   and de-veined
1 teaspoon sugar
salt to taste

For tempering:
3 tablespoons mustard oil
2 dried red chillies
2 bay leaves
1^1/$_2$ teaspoons whole Panch
   Phoran Spice Mix
   (see page 24)

Charchari means a mixture of three or four vegetables.
Here we have a non-vegetarian version with prawns alone.
Any mixed seafood can be used in the same recipe.

A traditional Muslim dish, these kebabs are simmered

in a *masala* (mixture) of spices and condiments.

Husseini Murg Masala

Husseini chicken curry

1 Arrange the chicken pieces, peppers and onions alternately on ten 15cm/6 inch skewers and set aside.

2 Heat the ghee or clarified butter in a pan, add the whole spices and let them splutter for 20 seconds. Add the onions and fry until brown.

3 Add the chilli powder, turmeric, yoghurt, ginger and garlic and stir-fry until the oil separates from the mixture. Then add the sugar and some salt to taste. Bring to the boil and simmer for 5 minutes.

4 Carefully add the skewers to the mixture and cook for 10–15 minutes, until the meat is tender and the sauce has a coating consistency. Serve in the sauce, or remove the skewers and serve the sauce separately.

Serves 4–6

1kg/2¼lb boneless chicken breasts, *cut into bite-sized pieces*
300g/11oz green peppers, *cut into bite-sized pieces*
300g/11oz red onion, *cut into bite-sized pieces*
125g/4½oz ghee or clarified butter *(see page 23)*
½ teaspoon cloves
1 teaspoon green cardamom pods
2 cinnamon sticks
2 bay leaves
250g/9oz onions, *finely chopped*
1 tablespoon red chilli powder
1 teaspoon ground turmeric
200g/7oz yoghurt, *preferably Greek yoghurt, whisked*
1 tablespoon Ginger Purée *(see page 22)*
1 tablespoon Garlic Purée *(see page 22)*
1 tablespoon sugar
salt to taste

Every Bengali's home-made favourite, this is a simple and superb way to cook fish.

Macher Jhol

Fish curry

1 Mix together half the turmeric, the ginger and garlic purées and some salt and then mix with the fish. Set aside for 20 minutes.

2 Heat the mustard oil in a pan, add the onion seeds and fry until they start to splutter. Then add the onions and fry for about 5 minutes, until they just start to turn brown. Add the fish and green chilli and fry for 2 minutes.

3 Mix the red chilli powder, remaining turmeric and some salt with 100ml/3^{1}/2fl oz water and add to the pan. Reduce the heat and simmer for 10 minutes, until the sauce thickens slightly, then stir in the lemon juice. Serve with steamed or boiled rice.

Serves 4–6

1^{1}/2 teaspoons ground
  turmeric
1 teaspoon Ginger Purée (see
  page 22)
1 teaspoon Garlic Purée (see
  page 22)
1kg/2^{1}/4lb cod or lemon sole
  fillet, skinned and cut into
  bite-sized pieces
100ml/3^{1}/2fl oz mustard oil

^{1}/4 teaspoon onion seeds
  (nigella seeds)
150g/5oz onions, thinly sliced
1 teaspoon finely chopped
  green chilli
1 teaspoon red chilli powder
1 teaspoon lemon juice
salt to taste

Bengal was once the hub of maritime commerce,

and this dish is well known in Malaysia, Singapore and Thailand.

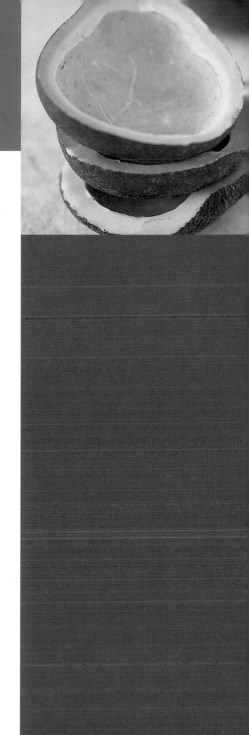

Chingri Malai Curry

Creamy prawn curry

Serves 4–6

1 coconut, freshly grated
600g/1lb 5oz medium-sized
   raw headless prawns,
   shelled
1/4 teaspoon ground turmeric
2 tablespoons mustard oil
2.5cm/1 inch piece of
   cinnamon stick

1 blade of mace
1 bay leaf
1 green chilli, seeded and
   finely chopped
1/2 teaspoon ground green
   cardamom
3 cloves, ground
salt to taste

1 Put the grated coconut in a piece of muslin and squeeze it over a bowl to extract the cream. Set the coconut cream aside. Then pour 1 1/2 cups of boiling water over the grated coconut, let it stand for 2 minutes and then squeeze in a piece of muslin again to extract the milk. Keep the cream and milk in different containers.

2 Mix the prawns with the turmeric and some salt and set aside for 10 minutes. Heat the mustard oil in a large pan, add the prawns and stir-fry over a high heat until they turn pink. Remove from the pan with a slotted spoon.

3 Add the cinnamon, mace and bay leaf to the oil in the pan and let them splutter for 10 seconds. Stir in the coconut milk and bring to the boil.

4 Add the prawns, chilli, ground cardamom, cloves and some salt. Simmer for 2 minutes, then stir in the coconut cream. This dish goes best with plain boiled rice.

People from as far away as Greece, Mesopotamia and Persia used to travel to Bengal to trade and this is just one of the fusion dishes that evolved from the interaction.

Keema Torkaari

Lamb-stuffed vegetables

1 Heat the oil in a pan until it reaches smoking point, add the cinnamon sticks and let them splutter for 15 seconds. Add the minced lamb and cook, stirring, until all the juices from the meat dry up.

2 Add the ground spices, onions, green chilli, sugar and some salt and cook, stirring, for 8–10 minutes. Pour in 1 litre/1¾ pints water and simmer until it has all been absorbed and the mixture is dry. Remove from the heat and leave to cool.

3 Prepare all the vegetables by slicing off a lid and making a cavity in each one (don't cut them in half), removing the pulp/seeds/flesh.

4 Fill the vegetables with the mince mixture and bake for 35–45 minutes in an oven preheated to 120°C/250°F/Gas Mark 1 or 2.

Serves 4–6

100ml/3½fl oz mustard oil
2 cinnamon sticks
1kg/2¼lb minced lamb
¼ teaspoon ground cloves
1 teaspoon ground green
  cardamom
½ teaspoon red chilli powder
1 teaspoon ground turmeric
250g/9oz onions, chopped
1 tablespoon finely chopped
  green chilli
2 teaspoons sugar
2 tomatoes

2 baby aubergines
2 green peppers
2 bitter gourds
2 snake gourds
salt to taste

The custom of preparing *Khitchuri* dates back to Aryan times, and many travellers to India have mentioned it in their travelogues. This method is truly time-tested!

Khitchuri

Kedgeree

Serves 4–6

100g/4oz rice
100g/4oz split green lentils
1 tablespoon mustard oil
$^1/_2$ teaspoon mustard seeds
$^1/_2$ teaspoon anise seeds
2 green chillies, chopped
1 teaspoon finely chopped
   fresh ginger
$^1/_4$ teaspoon ground turmeric
fried dried red chillies to
   serve, optional
salt to taste

1 Soak the rice and lentils in cold water for 30 minutes and then drain.

2 Heat the mustard oil in a pan, add the mustard seeds and anise seeds and let them splutter for 15 seconds. Then add the green chillies, ginger and turmeric and sauté for 30 seconds.

3 Pour in 400ml/14fl oz water and bring to the boil. Add the soaked rice and lentils and boil for 10 minutes.

4 Reduce the heat to very low, cover the pan and simmer for 15 minutes, until the rice and lentils are slightly overcooked and mushy. Season to taste with salt. Garnish with the chillies, if using.

Shobjee Jhalfarezi

Fried vegetables

1 Heat the mustard oil in a large pan until it reaches smoking point and add the whole spices. Let them splutter for 10 seconds, then add the potatoes and stir-fry for 2–3 minutes.

2 Add all the other vegetables and stir-fry for 3–4 minutes. Stir in the sugar and some salt, cover and cook on a very low heat for 10 minutes, until the vegetables are tender. Mix in the grated coconut, garnish with the coconut shavings and serve.

Serves 4-6

100ml/3½fl oz mustard oil
½ teaspoon Panch Phoran Spice Mix (see page 24)
2 bay leaves
100g/4oz potatoes, cut into fingers
100g/4oz wax gourd, cut into fingers
100g/4oz aubergine, cut into fingers
100g/4oz pumpkin, cut into fingers
1 large onion, cut into thick slices horizontally
1 large tomato, cut into thick slices horizontally
2 teaspoons sugar
5 tablespoons freshly grated coconut
toasted coconut shavings to serve
salt to taste

ERECTED TO COMMEMORATE THE LANDING
IN INDIA OF THEIR IMPERIAL MAJESTIES
KING GEORGE V AND QUEEN MARY

'Alphonso' is the king of Bombay mangoes – North India
has different varieties – and the best alphonsos come from
Ratnagiri, where a Mr Alphonso created the hybrid variety.

Mumbai

Bombay, now renamed Mumbai, on the Arabian Coast smells of the sea and of money. It is the commercial heart of India, home to the country's leading industrialists, to the matinee idols of Bollywood (the giant Hindi film industry), to murderous underworld dons as well as to a large homeless population. It teems with children of different gods – Hindu, Muslim, Sikh, Christian, Jew, Parsee. In the typical multi-layered identity of all Indians, these people are also Maratha, Gujarati, Parsee, Marwari, Anglo-Indian, Punjabi, Tamil, Malyali and Bihari. Bombay food is as diverse as its population and as complex as its history.

The original people to inhabit the group of seven islands that is modern Mumbai were the Koli fishermen. Then the rulers of Gujarat annexed the islands. In 1534 the Portuguese forced the Shah of Gujarat to transfer the islands to them and they called them Bom Baim – Good Harbour. In 1661, the English King Charles II married Catherine, sister of the Portuguese king, and she brought him Bombay in her dowry.

The gifts of the hot, tropical Arabian coast are the coconut, a huge variety of seafood and a good climate for growing fruit and vegetables, but each community developed its own distinctive cuisine. If the scholarly Brahmins are vegetarian, the warrior Marathas eat anything and one of their typical dishes is quails marinated in yogurt and spices, wrapped in wet clay and baked in an open fire.

The Koli fishing community eat very spicy food, cooked with coconut and green chillies, and use a special, pepper-like spice called chircoot for cooking fish. Fish such as newta, pomfret, surmai, prawns and crab are widely eaten. Even the Bombay duck is not duck at all but is dried fish.

Irani/Parsee restaurants popularised dishes such as *keema pao* (curried mince served with bread), *akuri* (made with eggs) and *patra* fish (baked in a banana leaf packet). The Bohri Muslim community developed their own distinctive style of cooking with dishes such as *palida* (thick broth) and *dabba-ghosht* (meat loaf). Mumbai's big Gujarati community is largely vegetarian, and they add a touch of sugar to most of their dishes.

Mumbai's street foods such as *bhel-poori* (a spicy dish of puffed rice, tamarind chutney, onions, green chillies), *pohe* (dry dish of pressed rice, onions and chillies), and *bhajjias* (made of onions or potatoes) are now eaten all over the country.

Fried fish is eaten more as a street snack in Bombay, and is especially popular all along the coast. Each seller selfishly guards the family recipe for the marinade mix.

Fried fish with aromatic spices; no dip is necessary as all the intended flavours are coated on the fish itself.

Tali Machi Masala

Fried fish

1 Mix together the turmeric, chilli powder, lemon juice, ginger and garlic purées and some salt. Spread this mixture over the fish fillets and set aside for 30 minutes.

2 Dust the fish in the plain flour, then in the rice flour and deep-fry in the vegetable oil for about 2 minutes, until crisp. Drain on kitchen paper and serve with a lemon wedge.

Serves 4–6

½ teaspoon ground turmeric
1 teaspoon red chilli powder
½ teaspoon lemon juice
½ teaspoon Ginger Purée (see page 22)
½ teaspoon Garlic Purée (see page 22)
1kg/2¼lb pomfret fillets (or other white fish fillets), skinned
100g/4oz plain flour
100g/4oz rice flour
1 litre/1¾ pints vegetable oil
lemon wedges to serve
salt to taste

The Parsee community in Bombay, originally from Persia, have cooked this family favourite for generations, and it is now enjoyed by all.

Murg Farcha

Fried chicken

Serves 4–6

1 chicken, skinned and cut
   into 8 pieces
1 tablespoon malt vinegar
1/2 teaspoon red chilli powder
a pinch of ground turmeric
Tamatar ki Chutney (Tomato
   chutney), to serve (see page
   133)
salt to taste

For frying:

4 eggs, lightly beaten
1/2 teaspoon Curry Powder
   (see page 23)
a pinch of red chilli powder
a pinch of ground turmeric
1 teaspoon finely chopped
   fresh mint
1 tablespoon finely chopped
   fresh coriander
1/2 teaspoon finely chopped
   green chilli
200g/7oz dried breadcrumbs
1 litre/1 3/4 pints vegetable oil

1 Mix the chicken pieces with the malt vinegar, chilli powder, turmeric and some salt and set aside for 1 hour. Place in a steamer and steam for 15 minutes, then leave to cool.

2 Mix together all the ingredients for frying except the breadcrumbs and oil. Coat the chicken pieces in this mixture and then roll them in the breadcrumbs. Repeat once more.

3 Deep-fry the chicken pieces in the hot oil until crisp and cooked through, then drain on kitchen paper and serve with some Tomato chutney.

This recipe is ideal for rejuvenating leftovers. Any vegetables or meat can be treated in the same way. Serve with naan bread.

Keema Par Anda

Spicy minced lamb with egg

1 Heat 100ml/3½fl oz of the oil in a large pan, add the cumin seeds and dried chillies and fry for 5 seconds. Add the onions and fry until golden brown.

2 Add the ginger, garlic, chilli powder, turmeric, tomatoes and some salt and cook, stirring, for about 10 minutes, until the oil separates from the mixture.

3 Add the minced lamb and cook for about 25 minutes, until all the juices from the meat have dried up and the oil has separated out again.

4 Heat the remaining oil in a frying pan and fry the eggs. Serve the mince garnished with the fried eggs.

Serves 4–6

125ml/4fl oz vegetable oil
½ teaspoon cumin seeds
6 small dried red chillies
150g/5oz onions, chopped
1 teaspoon finely chopped fresh ginger
1 teaspoon finely chopped garlic
½ teaspoon red chilli powder
⅓ teaspoon ground turmeric
100g/4oz tomatoes, chopped
1kg/2¼lb minced lamb
4 eggs
salt to taste

The Parsee community in Bombay love food and each
meal consists of endless courses, each a delight to savour.

A traditional Parsee recipe. The matchstick potatoes

can be bought ready to fry from Indian shops.

Salli Gosht

Lamb with straw potatoes

Serves 4–6

3 tablespoons vegetable oil

3 bay leaves

3 cloves

2 cinnamon sticks

½ teaspoon cumin seeds

4 tablespoons chopped onion

1kg/2¼lb boneless leg of lamb,
  cut into bite-sized pieces

1 tablespoon Ginger Purée
  (see page 22)

1 teaspoon Garlic Purée (see
  page 22)

5 fresh curry leaves

2 teaspoons red chilli powder

1 teaspoon ground coriander

200g/7oz tomatoes, chopped

2 tablespoons crushed jaggery

½ teaspoon Garam Masala
  (see page 24)

2 medium potatoes, peeled,
  cut into matchsticks and
  deep-fried until golden

1 tablespoon chopped fresh
  coriander (optional)

salt to taste

1 Heat the oil in a large pan and add the whole spices. Then add the onion and fry until golden brown.

2 Add the lamb, ginger and garlic purées, curry leaves, chilli powder, ground coriander and some salt and cook, stirring, for about 20 minutes, until the juices from the meat dry up.

3 Add the tomatoes and cook, stirring, for 10 minutes, then add 1 litre/1¾ pints water and the jaggery. Bring to the boil and simmer for 25 minutes, until the meat is tender and the sauce has thickened.

4 Stir in the garam masala, then sprinkle the matchstick potatoes, and chopped coriander if using, on top and serve.

Saar denotes a wet vegetable dish. It is ideal to eat

with rice or pooris (see page 131).

Tamatar, Phool Gobi, Gajjar Che Saar
Mixed vegetable curry

1 Heat the oil in a pan, add the mustard seeds and cumin seeds and let them crackle for 5 seconds. Then add the ginger, garlic, green chilli, curry leaves and chilli powder and sauté for 15 seconds.

2 Add the vegetables, sugar and some salt and stir-fry for 1 minute. Stir in the puréed tomatoes, bring to the boil and simmer until the vegetables are tender.

3 Stir in the coconut, coriander and ground black pepper and serve.

Serves 4–6

4 *tablespoons vegetable oil*
½ *teaspoon mustard seeds*
½ *teaspoon cumin seeds*
1 *teaspoon finely chopped fresh ginger*
1 *teaspoon finely chopped garlic*
1 *green chilli, finely chopped*
6 *fresh curry leaves*
¼ *teaspoon red chilli powder*
300g/11oz *prepared vegetables, such as mangetout, carrots, green beans, cauliflower, courgette, etc.*
a pinch of sugar
300g/11oz *fresh tomatoes, puréed*
2 *tablespoons grated coconut*
1 *tablespoon chopped fresh coriander*
¼ *teaspoon ground black pepper*
salt to taste

The curried aubergine rice goes very well with the *Bhindi ki Kadhi*.

Vanghi Bhaat

Rice with aubergine

1 Heat the vegetable oil in a large pan, add the cloves, mustard seeds and cinnamon sticks and cook for 10 seconds, until they start to crackle.

2 Add the aubergine, cashew nuts, asafoetida, turmeric and green chillies, and stir-fry for 2 minutes.

3 Add all the other ground spices, plus the yoghurt, rice, some salt and 750ml (1¼ pints) water. Bring to the boil, stir the rice once, and cook over a medium heat for 6–8 minutes, until the rice has absorbed all the water.

4 Reduce the heat to its lowest, cover the pan with a lid and cook for 20 minutes. Add the grated coconut and chopped coriander, mix well and serve.

Serves 4–6

3 tablespoons vegetable oil
4 cloves
½ teaspoon mustard seeds
2 cinnamon sticks
200g/7oz aubergine, cut into
    1cm/½ inch dice
12–15 cashew nuts
a pinch of asafoetida
½ teaspoon ground turmeric
2 green chillies, cut in half
½ teaspoon ground coriander
½ teaspoon ground cumin

⅓ teaspoon red chilli powder
2 tablespoons yoghurt,
    preferably Greek yoghurt,
    whisked
500g/1lb 2oz basmati rice
1 coconut, freshly grated
100g/4oz fresh coriander,
    chopped
salt to taste

Bhindi Ki Kadhi

Fried okra in sauce

1 Whisk together the yoghurt, gram flour and some salt and set aside. Heat the oil for deep-frying, add the okra and deep-fry over a medium heat until crisp. Remove and drain on kitchen paper.

2 Heat the vegetable oil in a pan, add the cumin seeds, onion seeds, dried chillies and asafoetida and fry for 10 seconds, until they begin to splutter. Add the onions and fry for about 10 minutes, until golden brown. Add the garlic purée and cook, stirring, for 1 minute.

3 Add the chilli powder and turmeric and cook, stirring, for 30 seconds. Then add the yoghurt mixture and bring to the boil. Reduce the heat and simmer for 20 minutes. Stir in the chopped coriander and fried okra and serve.

Serves 4–6

500g/1lb 2oz yoghurt,
    preferably Greek yoghurt,
    whisked
6 tablespoons gram flour
    (chickpea flour)
oil for deep-frying
1kg/2¼lb okra
5 tablespoons vegetable oil
½ teaspoon cumin seeds
a pinch of onion seeds (nigella
    seeds)
4 dried red chillies

a pinch of asafoetida
2 onions, chopped
1½ teaspoons Garlic Purée
    (see page 22)
½ teaspoon red chilli powder
½ teaspoon ground turmeric
4 tablespoons chopped fresh
    coriander
salt to taste

Grated raw mangoes transform the *Chitranna* into something truly memorable.

Coconut rice, or *Bhaat*, is made thoughout southern India, from Bombay to Cochin.

Chitranna

Mango rice

1 Heat 1 tablespoon of the oil in a pan, add the rice and stir-fry for 1 minute. Add 375ml/13fl oz water and bring to the boil. Simmer for about 10 minutes, until the rice has absorbed most of the water, then stir the rice carefully so as not to break the grains. Reduce the heat to very low, cover the pan, and cook for about 20 minutes longer, until the rice is tender. Set aside.

2 Heat the remaining oil in a wok. Add the mustard seeds, red chillies, asafoetida and turmeric and fry for 5 seconds. Add the black gram beans, roasted chana dal and peanuts and stir for 10 seconds.

3 Add the cooked rice, grated mango, sugar and some salt and mix well. Stir in the lemon juice.

Serves 4–6

3 tablespoons vegetable oil
250g/9oz basmati rice
1 teaspoon mustard seeds
5 dried red chillies
a pinch of asafoetida
a pinch of ground turmeric
2 teaspoons urad dal (black gram beans)
125g/4½oz roasted chana dal
3 tablespoons peanuts
2 tablespoons grated green unripe mango
½ teaspoon sugar
2 teaspoons lemon juice
salt to taste

Nariyal Bhaat

Coconut rice

1 Heat the oil in a casserole, add the mustard seeds and let them splutter for 5 seconds. Add the green chilli, ginger and curry leaves and fry for 15 seconds.

2 Add the rice and fry for 1 minute. Add the coconut milk and some salt and bring to the boil. Simmer until most of the coconut milk has been absorbed.

3 Cover the casserole with foil, transfer to an oven preheated to 200°C/400°F/Gas Mark 6 and bake for 20 minutes. Add the grated coconut and chopped coriander and mix well.

Serves 4–6

4 tablespoons vegetable oil
¼ teaspoon mustard seeds
¼ teaspoon finely chopped green chilli
½ teaspoon finely chopped fresh ginger
6 fresh curry leaves
250g/9oz basmati rice
375ml/13fl oz coconut milk
150g/5oz grated coconut
1 tablespoon chopped fresh coriander
salt to taste

Serve these tasty aubergines on a bed of turmeric rice – cook basmati rice in water to which turmeric powder has been added. This gives the rice a delicate yellow colour.

Vanghi

Spiced baby aubergines

1 Dry-roast the coconut and sesame seeds in a frying pan until golden brown. Set aside.

2 Heat half the oil in a pan, add the onion and fry until golden brown. Add all the spices, plus the roasted coconut and sesame seeds, the garlic, tamarind, jaggery, mango powder and some salt. Remove from the heat and grind to a smooth paste.

3 Slice the aubergines lengthways into quarters, leaving them attached at the stem. Apply some of the paste along the cut sides of the aubergines.

4 Heat the remaining oil in a large pan over a gentle heat and add the aubergines. Spread the remaining paste on top of them and cook for 8–10 minutes, until tender, adding a little water if necessary to make a sauce. Serve topped with the shreds of chilli.

Serves 4–6

6 tablespoons grated coconut
$^1/_2$ teaspoon sesame seeds
2 tablespoons vegetable oil
4 tablespoons chopped onion
1 teaspoon Goda Masala (see page 25)
$^1/_2$ teaspoon red chilli powder
$^1/_2$ teaspoon Garam Masala (see page 24)
2 garlic cloves, crushed
2 teaspoons tamarind paste
1 teaspoon crushed jaggery
$^1/_2$ teaspoon dried mango powder
250g/9oz baby aubergines
2 green chillies, deseeded and cut into fine julienne shreds
salt to taste

Goa's distinctive alcoholic feni, made from cashew nut and coconut, is said to have been distilled originally by monks.

Goa

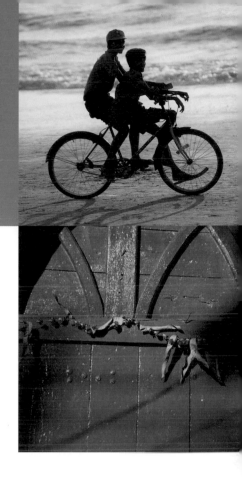

Goa is referred to as Gove – 'paradise' – in the *Puranas*, the ancient books of Indian wisdom. It is still a paradise, with long beaches, palm trees waving in the sea breeze and children selling fresh fruit on the beach, like useful cherubs. Tiny restaurants in beach shacks offer to cook fresh fish from the morning's catch. The juice of fresh *daab*, green coconut, completes the meal but on breezy moonlit nights the strong *feni*, coconut alcohol, can make the stars look much bigger and brighter.

Because of being on the Konkan coast, the main ingredients of cooking here are rice, fish, coconut and chillies. Fishermen set out to sea at dawn and return loaded with fresh fish – mackerel, pomfret and dozens of other varieties – that is sold then and there on the beach; a number of the fish sellers are women. The fish that remains unsold is dried in the hot sun.

Goan fish curries are legendary. Marinated in ground chilli paste, turmeric and vinegar, the fish could be fried, or stuffed and then fried. Prawn *balchao*, for example, is made with vinegar and chopped onions. The abundant coconut is used in full: its milk is used in cooking, its flesh is good for garnishes and coconut oil is the main cooking medium.

Goa was ruled by Hindus and then Muslims, followed by the Catholic Portuguese, so it became a land of Catholic churches, Hindu temples, Portuguese forts and mosques. A succession of Hindu dynasties ruled until 1472 A.D., when the Muslim Sultan of Bijapur took over. In 1510 A.D. the Portuguese commander Alfonso de Albuquerque conquered Goa. Albuquerque built a number of impressive buildings in old Goa, the most famous of which is the Basilica of Bom Jesus that houses the 360-year-old mummy of St Francis Xavier.

Goan cuisine reflects this intense mix of religions and cultures. The Mediterranean influence of the Portuguese is obvious in festive dishes such as roast suckling pig, also found in other Latin cultures. Pork is eaten in many forms, including sausages. *Sorpotel* is a fiery Goanese dish, traditionally made with pork cooked in vinegar. *Vindaloo* is another favourite dish, with more gravy than *sorpotel* and a little more sour. Garlic is used liberally, especially for *vindaloo* and *sorpotel*, when it is mixed with chillies and vinegar. Goan vinegar is made from toddy, which is distilled from the sap of palm trees.

Large raw prawns can be substituted for the lobster if preferred. Remove the head and shell

of each one and the dark intestinal vein running down the tail. Proceed as in step 4 below.

Jheenga Masala

Lobster in the shell

1 Kill the lobsters by plunging them into a very large pan of boiling salted water and boiling for 2 minutes. Drain well, then cut them lengthways in half, remove and discard the stomach sac from just behind the eyes and take out the dark intestinal vein running down the tail. Take out all the meat and reserve, discarding the gills. Cut the meat into large dice.

2 Heat the oil in a pan, add the carom seeds and let them crackle for 5 seconds. Add the ginger and garlic and fry until soft. Then add the onions and fry until they are limp but not coloured.

3 Dissolve the powdered rice in 150ml/¼ pint water. Add to the pan with the coconut cream, sugar, turmeric and some salt and bring to the boil. Simmer for 2 minutes.

4 Add the lobster and green chillies and cook for about 5 minutes, until the lobster is tender. Serve the lobster masala in the lobster shells with a boiled rice accompaniment.

Serves 4–6

2 large live lobsters
100ml/3½ fl oz vegetable oil
¼ teaspoon carom seeds
3 tablespoons finely shredded
fresh ginger
10 garlic cloves, sliced
2 onions, sliced
2 tablespoons raw rice,
ground to a powder
500ml/17fl oz coconut cream
1 tablespoon sugar
½ teaspoon ground turmeric
5 green chillies, cut into fine
shreds
salt to taste

This dish is one of the regulars eaten daily by Goanese. Many dishes in Goa have only

English or Portuguese names, reflecting their Portuguese legacy.

Goan Prawn Curry

1 Heat the oil in a heavy-based pan, add the onions and cook, stirring, for 3 minutes or until softened. Add the ginger and green chillies and cook for 1 minute.

2 Add the turmeric, coriander, chilli powder and cumin and mix well over a moderate heat. Dissolve the creamed coconut in 300ml/½ pint water. Stir it into the pan and cook until the oil separates from the mixture.

3 Add the tamarind and coconut milk, bring to the boil, then reduce the heat and simmer for 15 minutes.

4 Wash the prawns in cold water and drain thoroughly in a colander or sieve. Drop the prawns into the sauce, add some salt and simmer gently for about 5 minutes, until the prawns are cooked. The sauce should have a pouring consistency. Garnish with the coconut slivers, if using, and serve with steamed rice.

Serves 4–6

3 tablespoons vegetable oil
250g/9oz onions, thinly sliced
2 tablespoons chopped fresh
* ginger*
2 green chillies, finely chopped
a pinch of ground turmeric
1 teaspoon ground coriander
1 teaspoon red chilli powder
1 teaspoon ground cumin
50g/2oz creamed coconut
1 tablespoon tamarind paste
150ml/¼ pint coconut milk
800g/1¾lb medium-sized raw
* headless prawns, shelled*
* and de-veined*
slivers of coconut to garnish
* (optional)*
salt to taste

A typical Goan dish, this is also made with pork. *Vindaloo* is a Portuguese term for a dish made with vinegar and chillies.

Chicken Vindaloo

1 Mix together all the ground spices with some salt and rub them on to the chicken pieces. Set aside for 1 hour.

2 Heat the oil in a heavy-based pan and add the garlic purée. Stir-fry for 2 minutes, then add the onion purée. Stir-fry for 5 minutes, then add the ginger purée. Stir-fry for 2 minutes.

3 Add the chicken pieces and cook for 10 minutes. Stir in all the remaining ingredients and 150ml/¼ pint water and simmer for 10 minutes. The sauce should have reduced to a coating consistency. Serve with plain boiled rice.

Serves 4–6

a pinch of ground turmeric
½ teaspoon red chilli powder
1 teaspoon ground coriander
¼ teaspoon ground cinnamon
¼ teaspoon ground cloves
1 teaspoon ground cumin
½ teaspoon ground black pepper
600g/1lb 5oz boneless chicken, cut into bite-sized pieces
3 tablespoons vegetable oil
1 teaspoon Garlic Purée (see page 22)
300g/11oz Raw Onion Purée (see page 22)
1 teaspoon Ginger Purée (see page 22)
250g/9oz potatoes, peeled and cut into 2.5cm/1 inch cubes
1½ teaspoons sugar
3 tablespoons malt vinegar
3 tablespoons tomato purée
salt to taste

Bay leaves, cinnamon and cloves grow in abundance in Goa,

and were discovered by the Portuguese settlers, who created this hearty dish.

Lamb Assadu

Lamb with cinnamon and cloves

Serves 4–6

175ml/6fl oz vegetable oil
2 bay leaves
3 cloves
2.5cm/1 inch piece of
  cinnamon stick
1 teaspoon Garlic Purée (see
  page 22)
3 dried red chillies
300g/11oz onions, thickly
  sliced
1kg/2¼lb boneless leg of lamb,
  cut into 2.5cm/1 inch dice
½ teaspoon ground turmeric
1 teaspoon paprika
2 tablespoons malt vinegar
4 tomatoes, sliced
fresh bay leaves (optional)
salt to taste

1 Heat the oil in a large pan, add the bay leaves, cloves and cinnamon stick and let them splutter for a few seconds. Then add the garlic purée and dried red chillies and sauté for 10 seconds.

2 Add the onions and cook, stirring, for about 10 minutes, until golden brown. Add the lamb, turmeric, paprika and some salt and cook, stirring, for 15 minutes.

3 Pour in 500ml/17fl oz water and bring to the boil, then cover and simmer for 25 minutes.

4 Stir in the vinegar and cook until the sauce has reduced to a coating consistency. Arrange the tomato slices, and bay leaves if using, on top and serve with boiled rice.

Cafrael is the Portuguese term for chicken braised with
fresh mint, coriander and garlic.

Start the preparation the night before or on the morning you are cooking, to allow time for the marination of the chicken.

Chicken Cafrael

Serves 4–6

1kg/2¼lb boneless chicken thighs, cut into bite-sized pieces
1 litre/1¾ pints vegetable oil

For the marinade:

1 teaspoon Ginger Purée (see page 22)
1 teaspoon Garlic Purée (see page 22)
1 tablespoon Green Chilli Purée (see page 22)
½ teaspoon ground coriander
a pinch of ground cumin
a pinch of Garam Masala (see page 24)
100g (4oz) onions, roughly chopped
1 tablespoon tamarind paste
200g/7oz fresh coriander leaves
50g/2oz fresh mint leaves
½ teaspoon ground turmeric
2 tablespoons Cashew Nut Paste (see page 23)
3 tablespoons water
fresh mint leaves to garnish
salt to taste

1 Put all the ingredients for the marinade in a blender and process to a smooth paste. Marinate the chicken in the paste for at least 6 hours.

2 Heat the vegetable oil in a deep pan, add the chicken and deep-fry over a medium heat for about 10 minutes, until tender and cooked through. Remove from the pan, drain on kitchen paper, garnish with the mint leaves and serve straight away.

Ambotik denotes a home-made recipe for chicken or fish. The addition of tomatoes to the coconut-based gravy enhances the taste.

Ambotik

Chicken in coconut and onion gravy

1 Put the chopped onion, coriander, cumin, turmeric, paprika, chilli powder, some salt and 100ml/3½fl oz warm water in a blender and process to a paste.

2 Heat the vegetable oil in a heavy-based pan, add the sliced onion and fry for about 5 minutes, until golden brown. Then add the paste and fry over a medium heat for about 5 minutes, until the oil separates from the mixture. Add the tomatoes and cook, stirring, for 5 minutes.

3 Add the chicken pieces and some salt and cook, stirring, for 15 minutes. Reduce the heat and add 150ml/¼ pint water and the coconut milk. Cover and cook for 20 minutes, until the chicken is tender and the oil has separated from the mixture again.

4 Stir in the coconut cream. The sauce should have a pouring consistency. Serve with plain boiled rice.

Serves 4–6

2 onions, 1 chopped and
* 1 sliced*
1 teaspoon ground coriander
½ teaspoon ground cumin
½ teaspoon ground turmeric
1 tablespoon paprika
½ teaspoon red chilli powder
150ml/¼ pint vegetable oil
2 tomatoes, sliced
1kg/2¼lb boneless chicken,
* cut into bite-sized pieces*
100ml/3½fl oz coconut milk
200ml/7fl oz coconut cream
salt to taste

Balchao is a very warming dish, ideally served with chappatis or poories.

Any left over can be potted in ceramic jars, and is generally termed as pickle.

Prawn Balchao

Spiced prawns

Serves 4–6

5 tablespoons vegetable oil
6 cloves
2 cinnamon sticks
150g/5oz onions, sliced
1 tablespoon Garlic Purée (see page 22)
$\frac{1}{2}$ teaspoon red chilli powder
$\frac{1}{2}$ teaspoon crushed black pepper
$\frac{1}{2}$ teaspoon ground cumin
$\frac{1}{2}$ teaspoon ground fennel seed

3 tablespoons malt vinegar
350g/12oz tomatoes, chopped
15 fresh curry leaves
100g/4oz jaggery
1 tablespoon brown sugar
125g/4$\frac{1}{2}$oz tomato purée
1kg/2$\frac{1}{4}$lb medium-sized raw headless prawns, shelled and de-veined
salt to taste

1 Heat the oil in a deep, heavy-based pan or in a wok, add the cloves and cinnamon sticks and fry for 10 seconds, until they begin to splutter. Add the onions and cook, stirring, for 10 minutes, until they start to turn brown. Add the garlic purée and cook for 30 seconds.

2 Reduce the heat, add all the ground spices and the vinegar and cook until the oil starts to separate from the mixture.

3 Add the chopped tomatoes, curry leaves, jaggery, brown sugar and some salt and cook until the oil separates from the mixture again. Pour in 500ml/17fl oz water, bring to the boil and add the tomato purée. Mix well and simmer for about 15 minutes, until smooth.

4 Add the prawns and simmer for 6–8 minutes. Serve with plain boiled rice.

"मेरा जीवन ही मेरा संदेश है"

The impact of Moghlai cuisine on Hyderabad was so great
that pulaos and kebabs became very popular and led to
local variations, such as the famous Hyderabadi biryani.

Hyderabad

Hyderabad in Andhra Pradesh, one of the premier cities of India, was famous for its cuisine, wine and culture. Its rulers, the Nizams, were fabulously wealthy – the sixth Nizam, for example, had a 240-foot long wardrobe for his clothes. His son was the richest man in the world, with such quantity of treasure that he stored it in trucks parked in his palace grounds. Near Hyderabad are the famous Golconda diamond mines that yielded the fabled Koh-in-Noor, whose first owner was Mir Jumla, commander of the Hyderabad fort. When the fabulous gem passed into Moghul hands, Emperor Babur estimated its value at two-and-half days food for the entire world.

The Nizam, surrounded by immensely tall Pathan bodyguards, would sometimes come to eat at the humble cafés in town. These serve authentic Hyderabadi food, dishes such as *shorva* broths, made by simmering lamb bones or poultry in huge vats with vegetables, mint, coriander and spices; *nihari*, goat stew thickened with gramflour, cooked overnight in a sealed pot; piping hot lamb mince samosas; goat trotters (considered to be an aphrodisiac food) and a big choice of breads – *phulkas*, *kulchas*, *naan*, *tandoori parantha*, *aab-e-rawa* – many of which are cooked on charcoal fires. People on their way to work stop to eat a plate of *nihari* (lamb and lentil stew), with tandoori *roti*, for breakfast.

The eateries are close to the vegetable markets that begin trading at 4 a.m. as well as to the spice and meat markets. The penetrating smell of chillies, cumin, fenugreek, cardamom, vetiver, star aniseed and other spices, sold in open jute bags, pervades everything. In earlier times, the meat market sold live poultry since there were no refrigerators, but special cold rooms lined with ice were created for meat, including that of rabbit and camel.

Andhra food is hot and spicy and a recipe for mango pickle could, for example, call for equal weights of raw mango and red chillies. Tamarind is widely used. A typical Hyderabadi housewife's spicebox would include curry leaves, red chillies, mustard seeds, jaggery, peanuts, sesame seeds, cinnamon and cummin. Meat or vegetable dishes are garnished with a *baghar* where mustard and cumin seeds, curry leaves and red chillies are quickly fried in hot oil and poured over the simmering dish, after which it is swiftly covered to hold the flavour. The garnish helps to give it the authentic flavour of Hyderabad.

Add a tablespoon of chopped, fresh mint leaves just before serving to make this dish even more delectable.

Toasted melon seeds make an attractive garnish to this dish – just wash and dry

some melon seeds and then place under a medium-hot grill until lightly roasted.

Dal Gosht

Lamb and lentil curry

1 Soak the split peas in 1.5 litres/2½ pints water for 1 hour, then drain. Put the split peas in a pan with 1.5 litres/2½ pints fresh water and boil for 20 minutes, skimming off any scum from the top. Add the turmeric and some salt and boil for another 20 minutes.

2 Heat the vegetable oil in a large pan, add the whole spices and let them splutter for 10 seconds. Add the onions and stir-fry for 15 minutes, until golden brown.

3 Add the lamb, ginger and garlic purées, ground spices and some salt and cook, stirring, for 25 minutes.

4 Pour in 1 litre/1¾ pints water, bring to the boil and simmer for 20 minutes. Then add the split peas and cook, covered, on a very low heat for 20 minutes.

5 Heat the ghee or clarified butter in a pan, add the remaining tempering ingredients and let them splutter for 10 seconds. Pour this mixture on top of the cooked meat. Stir in the tamarind paste, coriander and green chilli and simmer for 10 minutes. Sprinkle on the melon seeds, if using, and serve.

Serves 4–6

550g/1¼lb channa dal
  (yellow split peas)
½ teaspoon ground turmeric
150ml/¼ pint vegetable oil
4 cinnamon sticks
1 teaspoon green cardamom
  pods
1 teaspoon cloves
4 teaspoons melon seeds
5 onions, chopped
1kg/2¼lb boneless leg of
  lamb, cut into 2.5cm/1 inch
  dice
2 tablespoons Ginger Purée
  (see page 22)
3 tablespoons Garlic Purée
  (see page 22)
1½ teaspoons red chilli
  powder
2 teaspoons ground cumin
½ teaspoon ground turmeric
50g/2oz tamarind paste
5 tablespoons chopped fresh
  coriander
1½ tablespoons finely
  chopped green chilli
salt to taste

For tempering:

50g/2oz ghee or clarified
  butter (see page 23)
8 dried red chillies
25 fresh curry leaves
1 tablespoon finely chopped
  garlic
½ teaspoon cumin seeds
¼ teaspoon fenugreek seeds
1 tablespoon toasted melon
  seeds to garnish (optional)

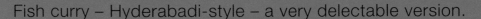
Fish curry – Hyderabadi-style – a very delectable version.

Machhli Ka Saalan

Hake in spiced coconut sauce

Serves 4–6

1 teaspoon red chilli powder
$^{1}/_{4}$ teaspoon ground turmeric
1 teaspoon tamarind paste
1 tablespoon ground
   coriander
1 teaspoon ground cumin
100ml/3$^{1}/_{2}$fl oz vegetable oil
150g/5oz onions, sliced
1 teaspoon Ginger Purée (see
   page 22)
1 teaspoon Garlic Purée (see
   page 22)
$^{1}/_{2}$ teaspoon Green Chilli
   Purée (see page 22)
150g/5oz tomatoes, chopped
500g/1lb 2oz hake fillet,
   skinned and cut into
   2.5cm/1 inch cubes
120ml/4fl oz coconut milk
slivers of fried garlic
1 tablespoon desiccated
   coconut
salt to taste

1 Put the chilli powder, turmeric, tamarind, ground coriander and cumin in a blender with 100ml/3$^{1}/_{2}$fl oz water and some salt and process to a purée.

2 Heat the oil in a pan, add the onions and fry until golden brown. Add the ginger, garlic and green chilli purées and the tomatoes and stir-fry for 2–3 minutes.

3 Add the tamarind mixture and stir-fry for another 2 minutes. Stir in 350ml/12fl oz water and bring to the boil.

4 Add the fish and simmer gently for 10 minutes. Stir in the coconut milk and heat through but do not let it boil. Sprinkle on the slivers of fried garlic and desiccated coconut and serve.

Hyderabadi cooking incorporates several aspects of Moghlai cuisine, but retains its own blend of ingredients.

Any Indian bread goes well with this dish.

Ande Ka Khagina

Scrambled eggs with chilli and coriander

1 Break the eggs into a bowl, add some salt and whisk for 30 seconds.

2 Heat the oil in a large pan, add the onions, green chilli, turmeric, chilli powder, ginger and garlic and stir-fry for 1 minute.

3 Add the eggs and scramble them, then cook until any moisture has dried up. Stir in the fresh coriander and serve.

Serves 4–6

10 eggs

4 tablespoons vegetable oil

200g/7oz onions, finely chopped

1 teaspoon finely chopped green chilli

a pinch of ground turmeric

¼ teaspoon red chilli powder

1 teaspoon Ginger Purée (see page 22)

1 teaspoon Garlic Purée (see page 22)

3 tablespoons chopped fresh coriander

salt to taste

During the fasting season of Holy Ramzan, Muslims eat *Haleem* before sunrise – it is considered to be very nourishing.

Haleem

Spiced lamb with wheat

1 Mix together the lamb, yoghurt, ginger and garlic purées and some salt and set aside for 2 hours.

2 Soak the broken wheat in 1 litre/1¾ pints water for 1 hour, then drain, put in a pan and cover with fresh water. Bring to the boil and simmer for about 20 minutes, until tender. Drain off excess water through a sieve.

3 Heat the ghee in a large, heavy-based pan, add the onions and fry for about 15 minutes, until golden brown. Add the meat and cook, stirring, for 20–25 minutes, until all the natural juices dry up and the oil separates from the mixture.

4 Add the ground spices and cook for another 5 minutes, then add 1.5 litres/2½ pints water. Bring to the boil and simmer, covered, for 30 minutes, stirring every 5 minutes.

5 Remove half the meat from the pan and set aside. Add the boiled wheat to the remaining meat and cook on a very low heat, mashing the lamb and broken wheat constantly with a wooden spoon (or you can purée the mixture in a blender).

6 Put the cashew nuts, desiccated coconut and poppy seeds in a blender with 100ml/3½fl oz water and blend to a paste. Add this to the pan with the reserved meat and continue cooking for 10–15 minutes. The mixture should have the consistency of porridge. Stir in the lemon juice and serve, garnished with the coriander, mint and fried cashew nuts.

Serves 4–6

500g/1lb 2oz boneless
   shoulder or leg of lamb, cut
   into 2.5cm/1 inch cubes
4 tablespoons yoghurt,
   preferably Greek yoghurt,
   whisked
2 teaspoons Ginger Purée (see
   page 22)
1 tablespoon Garlic Purée (see
   page 22)
250g/9oz daliya (broken
   wheat or bulghur wheat)
100g/4oz ghee (see page 23)
250g/9oz onions, thinly sliced
1 teaspoon red chilli powder
¼ teaspoon ground cloves
½ teaspoon ground cinnamon
1 teaspoon ground green
   cardamom
40g/1½oz cashew nuts
25g/1oz desiccated coconut
1 teaspoon poppy seeds
1 tablespoon lemon juice
salt to taste

To garnish:

2 tablespoons chopped fresh
   coriander
1½ teaspoons chopped fresh
   mint
25–30 cashew nuts, fried

Shiny purple aubergines are twice cooked – once in hot oil and then simmered in

a sweet/sour sauce. Jaggery (below right) is sugarcane juice that is crystallised into solids.

Baghare Baingan

Aubergines in piquant sauce

1 Cut the aubergines lengthways in half but leave them attached at the stem. Heat the oil for deep-frying over a moderate heat, add the aubergines and fry for 15 minutes. Remove and leave to drain on kitchen paper.

2 Dry-roast the onions in an oven preheated to 220°C/425°F/Gas Mark 7 for 30 minutes, until the skin is blackened. Peel off the top layer of each onion and set aside.

3 Heat a heavy-based frying pan over a medium heat, add all the whole spices except the mustard seeds and dry-roast for 5 minutes. Grind to a powder.

4 Put the ground roasted spices in a blender with the roasted onions, coconut, ginger and garlic purées, jaggery, peanuts, tamarind, turmeric, chilli powder and some salt and blend to a smooth paste, adding up to 100ml/3 ^{1}/2fl oz water if necessary.

5 Heat the vegetable oil in a pan, add the mustard seeds and let them crackle for 10 seconds. Then add the curry leaves and cook, stirring, for 5 seconds. Add the prepared paste and stir over a low heat for 10 minutes, until the oil separates from the mixture.

6 Pour in 250ml/8fl oz water and bring to the boil. Add the aubergines and simmer for 5 minutes. Check the seasoning and serve garnished with deep-fried shreds of leek.

Serves 4–6

500g/1lb 2oz baby aubergines
oil for deep-frying
2 onions
2 teaspoons coriander seeds
1 teaspoon cumin seeds
^{1}/2 teaspoon sesame seeds
^{1}/2 teaspoon poppy seeds
5–6 fenugreek seeds
4 tablespoons desiccated
*   coconut*
2 tablespoons Ginger Purée
*   (see page 22)*
1 tablespoon Garlic Purée (see
*   page 22)*
50g/2oz jaggery
2 tablespoons peanuts
2^1/2 tablespoons tamarind
*   paste*
^{1}/4 teaspoon ground turmeric
^{1}/2 teaspoon red chilli powder
5 tablespoons vegetable oil
^{1}/2 teaspoon black mustard
*   seeds*
15–20 fresh curry leaves
1 leek, shredded and deep
*   fried*
salt to taste

This dish is welcome during the monsoon season, since stored green tomatoes last for months and there is no need to visit the market, which can be many miles away.

Tamatar Waale Chaawal

Tomato rice

1 Soak the rice in 2 litres/3½ pints water for 1 hour, then drain.

2 Finely chop half the tomatoes and cut the rest into quarters. Heat the oil in a heavy-based pan, add the finely chopped tomatoes, chilli powder, green chillies, ginger and some salt and stir-fry for 5 minutes.

3 Add 900ml/1½ pints water and bring to the boil. Add the soaked rice and tomato quarters and bring back to the boil. Cook, stirring gently, for about 10 minutes, until the water has been absorbed.

4 Reduce the heat to very low, cover the pan with a tight-fitting lid and cook for 15–20 minutes. Sprinkle over the lemon juice, mix into the rice and serve.

Serves 4–6

500g/1lb 2oz basmati rice
200g/7oz tomatoes
100ml/3½ fl oz vegetable oil
1 teaspoon red chilli powder
2 green chillies, cut in half
2 tablespoons finely shredded fresh ginger
4 teaspoons lemon juice
salt to taste

Not only full of flavours and textures, this dish is rich in protein.

Saag Dal

Spinach with mung beans

Serves 4–6

500g/1lb 2oz moong dal
  (yellow mung beans)
1/2 teaspoon ground turmeric
1 tablespoon Ginger Purée
  (see page 22)
2 tablespoons Garlic Purée
  (see page 22)
5 green chillies, cut in half
500g/1lb 2oz baby spinach,
  washed
2 tablespoons lemon juice
2 tablespoons dried mango
  powder
100g/4oz fresh coriander,
  chopped
salt to taste

For tempering:

120ml/4fl oz vegetable oil
1/2 teaspoon mustard seeds
1/2 teaspoon cumin seeds
4 dried red chillies
25–30 fresh curry leaves
1 tablespoon chopped garlic

1 Soak the mung beans in 1 litre/1¾ pints water for
30 minutes, then drain. Heat 1.5 litres/2½ pints water in a large
pan, add the drained mung beans and bring to the boil. Boil for
10 minutes, then skim the scum from the top.

2 Add the turmeric, ginger and garlic purées, green chillies and
some salt and simmer for 20 minutes. Keep simmering while you
prepare the tempering.

3 Heat the vegetable oil in a pan, add the mustard seeds, cumin
seeds and dried red chillies and let them crackle for a few
seconds. Then add the curry leaves and garlic and stir-fry for
10 seconds. Add the spinach and sauté for 30 seconds. Add this
mixture to the mung beans and simmer for 5 minutes. Stir in the
lemon juice, mango powder and chopped coriander, and serve.

The medley of racial, religious and cultural influences in South India has resulted in a profusion of superb culinary styles.

Chennai

The Coromandel Coast on the east and the Malabar Coast on the western strip of South India are home to the country's most ancient race, the Dravidians, but international trade by sea was always brisk and many ancient foreigners settled there. Traders came for sesame oil, sandal, betel, muslin that was described as 'webs of woven wind', salt, pepper and other spices. The ancient Romans, Greeks and Arabs came by sea, the Dutch, French, Portuguese and English followed. The majority of the inhabitants are Hindus but there are big populations of Christians and Muslims and each community has its own cuisine. Syrian Christians eat beef, Kerala Muslims eat meat biryani and harisa (a broth of ground wheat and meat), the Hindu Nair specialities are *aviyal* (vegetables in coconut milk) and chicken cooked in coconut, the Hindu Namboodiri Brahmins, custodians of the ancient knowledge of Ayurveda, are strict vegetarians who eat rice *idli* and *dosai* for breakfast.

Ayurvedic cures involve diet, herbs, yoga and meditation. The doctor deals with the three biological humors – *Vata*, *Pitta*, *Kapha*, i.e. air, fire and water – which determine the forces of growth and decay in the body. Accordingly, heating and cooling foods are prescribed. The most heating foods are generally pungent, followed by sour and salty. The most cooling taste is bitter, followed by astringent and sweet. Eating sweets harmonises the mind and promotes contentment. Salty food works as a laxative and sedative. The sour taste is both carminative and a stimulant. Bitter foods purify and detoxify. Astringent foods stop bleeding and help heal skin and mucus membrane.

Madras, which has reverted back to its old name Chennai (Beautiful City), was famous for its Udipi cuisine. The hot and sour *rassam* soup (see page 115) has always been part of the meal. In the 17th century, the English saw the Brahmin Tamil yogis drinking *mulagu-thanni* (pepper water) and adapted the concept to create mulligatawny soup. Tiffin, a light meal, was another notion adopted by the British.

South Indian food is spicy – hot food makes you sweat, thus cooling the body. Food is commonly spiced with pepper, dried red chillies, cinnamon, cloves and star anise, and flavoured with fresh curry leaves, garlic and coconut. Cooking time for vegetables is very short and everything is eaten with rice. Banana, yam, jackfruit and cassava grown in abundance. Meals are traditionally eaten on fresh green banana leaves, and apart from coffee, the fermented Toddy and local port wine are widely drunk.

Locally known as *mulagu-tanni* (pepper water), this British Raj creation was originally

peppercorns simmered in water with coriander, salt and turmeric – a common pick-me-up.

Mulagu-Tanni

Mulligatawny soup

1 Boil the drained soaked split peas in 2 litres/3½ pints water with the turmeric for about 1 hour, until they are completely soft. Transfer to a blender and purée until smooth.

2 Heat the oil in a pan, add the ginger, garlic, curry leaves, coconut, curry powder and two-thirds of the apples and sauté for 6–8 minutes. Add the split pea purée, coconut milk and 150ml/¼ pint water and bring to the boil. Simmer for 20 minutes.

3 Remove from the heat and pass through a fine sieve. Return to the pan and simmer for 10 minutes. Stir in the coconut cream and lemon juice and season to taste. Add the remaining apple cubes and garnish with the curry leaves.

Serves 4–6

400g/14oz channa dal (yellow split peas), soaked in cold water for 2 hours, then drained
½ teaspoon ground turmeric
100ml/3½ fl oz vegetable oil
1½ teaspoons finely chopped fresh ginger
1 teaspoon finely chopped garlic
10–12 fresh curry leaves

4 tablespoons desiccated coconut
1½ teaspoons Curry Powder (see page 23)
3 cooking apples, peeled, cored and cut into 2.5cm/1 inch dice
150ml/¼ pint coconut milk
2 tablespoons coconut cream
2 tablespoons lemon juice
curry leaves to garnish
salt to taste

This soup can be eaten as a starter,

or boiled rice can be added to it to make a main course dish.

Thakkali Rassam

Thin tomato soup

1 Heat 1 tablespoon of the oil in a pan, add the green chilli and garlic purées and sauté for 10 seconds. Then add the tomatoes and cook, stirring, for 1 minute.

2 Stir in the turmeric, chilli powder and 2 litres/3½ pints water. Bring to the boil, reduce the heat to very low and simmer for 30 minutes.

3 Heat the remaining oil in a small pan, add the asafoetida and curry leaves and stir for 10 seconds. Add this mixture to the simmering tomatoes, then stir in the fresh coriander, black pepper and some salt and cook for 10 minutes.

4 Remove from the heat and leave to stand for 2 minutes, until all the sediment has settled down. With a ladle, remove all the liquid from the top with the coriander and curry leaves – only this liquid should be served.

Serves 4–6

2 tablespoons vegetable oil
1 green chilli, seeded
½ teaspoon Garlic Purée (see
    page 22)
1kg/2¼lb tomatoes, cut into
    quarters
a pinch of ground turmeric
¼ teaspoon red chilli powder
a pinch of asafoetida
8 fresh curry leaves
1 teaspoon chopped fresh
    coriander
¼ teaspoon ground black
    pepper
salt to taste

Nilgiris is the name of a mountain range where herbs and spices grew

in abundance; the local people used them all to tasty effect in this curry.

Lemon Rice

400g/14oz basmati rice
100ml/3½fl oz coconut oil
4–5 dried red chillies
½ teaspoon mustard seeds
1 cinnamon stick
4 cloves
a pinch of asafoetida
2 tablespoons peanuts
2 tablespoons cashew nuts
½ teaspoon urad dal (black gram
    beans)
1 tablespoon chopped fresh ginger
¼ teaspoon ground turmeric
10–12 fresh curry leaves
4 tablespoons desiccated coconut
2 tablespoons lemon juice
salt to taste

1 Soak the rice in cold water for 30 minutes, then drain. Put it in a pan with 2 litres/3½ pints salted water and boil for 8–10 minutes. It should be slightly undercooked. Drain well and set aside.

2 Heat the oil in a pan, add the whole spices, asafoetida, peanuts, cashew nuts and black gram beans and let them splutter for 15 seconds. Add the ginger, turmeric and curry leaves and stir-fry for 10 seconds. Stir in the boiled rice, desiccated coconut and some salt and toss until the rice is thoroughly heated. Do this gently or the grains of rice will break. Sprinkle over the lemon juice, mix well and serve.

Nilgiri Korma

Nilgiri lamb korma

1 Put the ginger, garlic, green chillies, coriander, mint and 250ml/8fl oz water in a blender and process to a smooth paste, then set aside. Put the fried cashew nuts in the blender with 150ml/¼ pint water and purée, then set aside.

2 Heat the oil in a pan, add the whole spices and let them crackle for 10 seconds. Then add the onions and fry until golden brown.

3 Add the meat, ground coriander, chilli powder, desiccated coconut and some salt and cook, stirring, for about 20 minutes, until all the juices from the meat dry up.

4 Reduce the heat, add the green paste and cashew nut paste and cook, stirring, for about 20 minutes, until the oil separates from the mixture.

5 Pour in the coconut milk and 1 litre/1¾ pints water. Bring to the boil and simmer for 25 minutes, then stir in the garam masala. Garnish with the ginger strips and serve.

Serves 4–6

1 tablespoon chopped fresh
    ginger
2 tablespoons chopped garlic
2 green chillies, seeded and
    chopped
200g/7oz fresh coriander
100g/4oz fresh mint
100g/4oz cashew nuts, fried
150ml/¼ pint vegetable oil
1 cinnamon stick
6 cloves
1 star anise
200g/7oz onions, sliced
1kg/2¼lb boneless leg of
    lamb, cut into bite-sized
    pieces
1 teaspoon ground coriander
½ teaspoon red chilli powder
150g/5oz desiccated coconut
150ml/¼ pint coconut milk
¼ teaspoon Garam Masala
    (see page 24)
large knob of fresh ginger, cut
    into julienne strips
salt to taste

South Indian cooking traditionally uses peppercorns for heat,
and chillies have only been included for the past 400 years.

English names for ingredients are fairly common in South India – a legacy of the British Raj – hence this dish is called the same in Tamil.

Coconut Lamb Fry

Lamb with coconut and coriander

1 Heat the coconut oil in a pan, add the mustard seeds and fenugreek seeds and let them splutter for 15 seconds. Add the onions and cook, stirring, for 10 minutes or until golden brown.

2 Add the curry leaves, turmeric, ginger, garlic, green chilli, ground coriander, lamb and some salt. Cook, stirring, over a low heat for 20–25 minutes, until all the juices from the meat have dried up.

3 Add the tomatoes and coconut milk and cook until the oil separates from the mixture. Stir in the desiccated coconut and fresh coriander. Serve with bread.

Serves 4–6

150ml/¼ pint coconut oil
½ teaspoon mustard seeds
6–8 fenugreek seeds
150g/5oz onions, chopped
10–12 fresh curry leaves
½ teaspoon ground turmeric
2 teaspoons finely chopped
  fresh ginger
1 teaspoon finely chopped
  garlic
½ teaspoon finely chopped
  green chilli
1 teaspoon ground coriander
1kg/2¼lb boneless leg of
  lamb, cut into bite-sized
  pieces
100g/4oz fresh tomatoes,
  puréed
150ml/¼ pint coconut milk
150g/5oz desiccated coconut
2 tablespoons chopped fresh
  coriander
salt to taste

Madras has an abundance of coconut trees, and fresh coconut flesh,

diced or shredded, is used rather than desiccated coconut.

Ginger Chicken

1 Heat the sesame oil and vegetable oil in a pan, add the onion seeds and let them crackle for 10 seconds. Add the rassampatti chillies and cook for 10 seconds, then add the onions and stir-fry for 5 minutes, until golden brown.

2 Add the ginger, curry leaves, green chilli, chicken, turmeric and some salt and cook, stirring, for 10 minutes.

3 Add the tomatoes and cook, stirring, for another 10 minutes. Add the honey and chopped coriander, mix well and serve.

Serves 4–6

60ml/2fl oz sesame oil
100ml/3½fl oz vegetable oil
a pinch of onion seeds (nigella seeds)
6 rassampatti chillies or other hot dried red chillies
150g/5oz onions, chopped
1 tablespoon chopped fresh ginger
10 fresh curry leaves
1 teaspoon seeded and finely chopped green chilli

1kg/2¼lb boneless chicken, cut into bite-sized pieces
a pinch of ground turmeric
100g/4oz tomatoes, chopped
¼ teaspoon honey
2 teaspoons chopped fresh coriander
salt to taste

Sambhar

Sour lentil curry with vegetables

1 Soak the lentils in 1 litre/1¾ pints water for 30 minutes, then drain and put them in a pan with 600ml/1 pint fresh water. Add the turmeric, bring to the boil and simmer for 30 minutes, until tender.

2 Heat the oil in a separate pan, add the mustard seeds and let them crackle for 10 seconds. Add the curry leaves and asafoetida and stir for 10 seconds.

3 Add the vegetables, sambhar powder and some salt and sauté for 2 minutes. Add the cooked lentils, tamarind paste, jaggery and grated coconut, bring to the boil and simmer for 10 minutes.

Serves 4–6

200g/7oz toor dal (large yellow lentils)
½ teaspoon ground turmeric
5 tablespoons vegetable oil
½ teaspoon mustard seeds
10 fresh curry leaves
2 pinches of asafoetida
1 green drumstick, cut into 2.5cm/1 inch pieces
1 onion, cut into 2.5cm/1 inch dice
2 tomatoes, cut into quarters
2 baby aubergines, cut into quarters
2 tablespoons diced pumpkin, preferably white, in 2.5cm/ 1 inch cubes

4 okra, cut in half
2 tablespoons Sambhar Powder (see page 24)
2½ teaspoons tamarind paste
1cm/½ inch piece of jaggery
2 tablespoons grated fresh coconut
salt to taste

Outdoor cooking, especially in hill districts, is popular in summer. The British termed them as 'camp tiffins'.

Pepper is used extensively in southern India, where temperatures are high.

It helps to lower body temperature by making you drink more water.

Chicken Pepper Fry

1 Heat the coconut oil in a pan, add the cumin seeds and mustard seeds and let them splutter for 5 seconds. Add the onions and stir-fry for 10 minutes, until they start to turn brown.

2 Add the ginger and garlic purées, the green chilli and the curry leaves and stir-fry for 2 minutes. Add the chicken, ground coriander, turmeric, cumin and some salt and stir-fry for 5 minutes.

3 When the juices from the chicken have dried up, add the tomatoes and stir-fry for 5 minutes. Simmer over a gentle heat for about 10 minutes, until the oil separates from the mixture and the liquid dries up. Stir in the lemon juice and crushed black pepper, then serve with bread.

Serves 4–6

100ml/3½fl oz coconut oil
½ teaspoon cumin seeds
½ teaspoon mustard seeds
200g/7oz onions, chopped
2 teaspoons Ginger Purée (see page 22)
1 teaspoon Garlic Purée (see page 22)
1 teaspoon finely chopped green chilli
10–12 fresh curry leaves
1kg/2¼lb boneless chicken, cut into bite-sized pieces
1 teaspoon ground coriander
½ teaspoon ground turmeric
½ teaspoon ground cumin
150g/5oz tomatoes, chopped
1 tablespoon lemon juice
½ teaspoon crushed black pepper
salt to taste

The Malabar sea coast boasts the longest stretch of beach in the world – spanning nearly six states.

The coconut palms of India's coastline provide the coconut oil and milk so often used in Indian cookery.

Here, fresh prawns are combined with the flavour of coconut to make a very quick and tasty meal.

Malabar Prawn Curry

1 Heat the coconut oil on a low heat, add the whole spices and let them splutter for 15 seconds. Add the onion and sauté for 5 minutes, until it becomes limp and starts to change colour.

2 Stir in the ginger, garlic, green chilli and curry leaves and sauté for 2 minutes. Add the puréed tomato, ground spices and some salt and sauté until the oil separates from the mixture.

3 Push a small bamboo stick through the length of each prawn to keep them straight while they are cooking. Add the prawns to the mixture and stir-fry over a high heat for 2 minutes. Then add the coconut milk and bring to the boil.

4 Simmer for 1 minute, then remove from the heat and stir in the coconut cream. Serve with rice.

Serves 4–6

150ml/ ¼ pint coconut oil
6 green cardamom pods
5 cloves
3 cinnamon sticks
5 tablespoons finely chopped onion
1 teaspoon finely chopped fresh ginger
1 teaspoon finely chopped garlic
½ teaspoon finely chopped green chilli
8–10 fresh curry leaves
5 tablespoons puréed fresh tomato
½ teaspoon ground coriander
¼ teaspoon red chilli powder
¼ teaspoon ground turmeric
1kg/2¼lb raw prawns, shelled but leaving tails on, cleaned and de-veined
8 tablespoons coconut milk
3 tablespoons coconut cream
salt to taste

Sesame Rice

250g/9oz basmati rice
1 tablespoon sesame oil
2 tablespoons vegetable oil
¼ teaspoon black sesame seeds
1 tablespoons crushed peanuts
salt to taste

1 Soak the rice in 1 litre/ 1¾ pints cold water for 30 minutes, then drain well and set aside.

2 Heat the sesame oil and vegetable oil in a pan, add the sesame seeds and crushed peanuts and let them crackle for 5 seconds. Add the drained rice and stir for 1 minute.

3 Add 375ml/13fl oz water, bring to the boil and simmer until the rice has absorbed most of the water. Cover with foil, place in an oven preheated to 200°C/400°F/Gas Mark 6 and cook for 25 minutes.

Poriyal literally means 'stir-fry' in Tamil. All leafy vegetables can be prepared in this manner. Madras Potatoes are eaten with rice pancakes, *dosa*, for breakfast in Madras.

Cabbage Poriyal

1 Heat the coconut oil on a low heat, add the black gram beans, cumin and mustard seeds and let them crackle for 15 seconds. Add the onions and stir-fry for 5 minutes, until they are limp but not coloured.

2 Add the ginger, garlic, curry leaves and green chilli and sauté for 1 minute. Raise the heat and add the cabbage and some salt. Stir-fry until the cabbage is hot but still crisp. Be careful that it doesn't start to give off any liquid; if it does, cook until it has evaporated.

3 Add the desiccated coconut, chopped coriander and lemon juice and mix well.

Serves 4–6

5 tablespoons coconut oil
1/2 teaspoon urad dal (black gram beans)
1/2 teaspoon cumin seeds
1/2 teaspoon black mustard seeds
150g/5oz onions, chopped
2 teaspoons finely chopped fresh ginger
1 teaspoon finely chopped garlic
10–12 fresh curry leaves
1/2 teaspoon finely chopped green chilli
1kg/2 1/4lb white cabbage, shredded
8 tablespoons desiccated coconut
4 tablespoons chopped fresh coriander
1 tablespoon lemon juice
salt to taste

Madras Potatoes

1 Boil the potatoes in salted water with the turmeric until they are just cooked but still a little crunchy. Drain well.

2 Heat the vegetable oil in a large pan, add the potatoes and deep-fry over a low heat until crisp. Remove the potatoes from the pan and leave on kitchen paper to drain.

3 Heat the coconut oil in a large pan, add the mustard seeds and let them crackle for 5 seconds. Then add the curry leaves and fry for 5 seconds.

4 Stir in the chilli powder and cumin and fry for 2 seconds. Add the potatoes and toss them in the spices, then stir in the chopped coriander and lemon juice.

Serves 4–6

500g/1lb 2oz small new potatoes, peeled and cut in half
a pinch of ground turmeric
1 litre/1 3/4 pints vegetable oil
2 tablespoons coconut oil
1/4 teaspoon black mustard seeds
6 fresh curry leaves
2 pinches of red chilli powder
1/2 teaspoon ground cumin
2 tablespoons chopped fresh coriander
1/2 teaspoon lemon juice

Vegetables form a major part of South Indian meals – numerous
varieties are sold each day from woven palmleaf baskets,
precariously perched on the padded heads of the hawkers.

In India, no marriage ceremony is complete without the bride feeding the groom a sweetmeat – and vice versa.

Breads, Chutneys and Sweets

Good to eat at any time, these accompaniments are extremely popular in India and, as with other dishes, they vary from region to region.

In India breads are planned and baked with consideration for the occasion and mood. *Pooris* are usually eaten for lunch, *chappatis* or *rotis* accompany a hearty meal, filled *naans* are eaten as snacks, and sweet breads are for celebrations. Almost all restaurants in Northern India have a tandoor oven, and bake their breads to order. Since most Indian bread is unleavened and rolled out flat, it cooks quickly, and in most Indian homes the *roti* is cooked when the meal is being served so that it it eaten hot.

Chutneys play a major part in any meal in India. They can either be made fresh – with any available ingredients such as roast lentils, roast sesame seeds, fresh coriander, coconut or even onions – or, if cooked, they can be potted. Potted chutneys are long lasting and are made from ingredients such as mangoes, garlic, tomatoes, aubergines, limes, lemons or mixed vegetables.

The spices used in every chutney are particular to it and are chosen to enhance the flavour of that particular fruit or vegetable; for example ajwain spice is used in oily chutney to help digest the oil; lentil-based chutneys include asafoetida to prevent gastric problems; and winter chutneys call for green chillies or black pepper which help to give some immunity against winter colds.

Sweets are the food of the gods. Benares, city of gods, has a huge variety and some such as *malai poori* (thick cream served like a pancake on a leaf plate) are particular to that city. In Punjab sweets tend to be rich, such as *halwa*; Bengalis use *chenna* (cottage cheese) and date palm molasses; and Goan housewives use a great deal of coconut in their sweets. Parsee sweets such as *malai na khaja* (a type of baklava) reflect their Persian origins, while *kulfi* (Indian ice cream) was popular with Moghuls but today is widely eaten all over India.

Breads

Bread is an essential part of every meal for nearly half the population of India – a staggering 530 million people. The rest are rice eaters.

The bread eaten in India today is almost the same as the bread baked for ancient rulers, with the same basic ingredients being used – flour, water and a leavening agent. Although India has western-style bread, called *double-roti*, the word 'bread' is not really appropriate for the dozens of varieties of *rotis* eaten all over the country.

The oldest Indian *roti* is the flat tandoori *roti*, which for over five thousand years has been baked in the tandoor oven. Tandoori *roti*, tandoori *parantha* and *naan* have always been popular, but *rotis* are also fried and roasted, such as the immensely popular *pooris* and *paranthas*. *Poori-aloo* (*poori* with potato curry) is a meal in itself, as is stuffed *parantha* with yogurt and pickle. *Pooris* can be stuffed with lentils and spices, and are deep-fried in a *kadai* (deep wok); *paranthas* can be stuffed with almost anything and are shallow-fried on a *taiwa* (iron griddle).

Rotis can also be sweet. Peshawari *naan*, for example, is a sweet *naan* made with cardamom and nuts. Sweet *paranthas*, layered with sugar that melts during cooking, are popular with children.

Naan

Leavened flat bread

1 Put the flour, salt and bicarbonate of soda in a bowl and mix well. Whisk together the yoghurt, milk, sugar and egg and mix with the flour to form a soft dough. Turn out on to a lightly floured surface and knead for 3 minutes.

2 Add the oil and knead for another 2 minutes, then cover with clingfilm and chill for 30 minutes.

3 Divide the dough into 15 balls and dot each one with the onion seeds. Flatten the dough balls with your hand and stretch into 'tear-drop' shapes (or roll out into ovals with a rolling pin), about 5mm/¼ inch thick.

4 Cook in an oven preheated to 240°C/475°F/Gas Mark 9 for 5–7 minutes, or in a hot tandoor oven for 2 minutes, until the *naan* are soft, fluffy and patched with brown.

Serves 4–6

250g/9oz plain white flour
a pinch of salt
¼ teaspoon bicarbonate of
    soda
1 tablespoon yoghurt,
    preferably Greek yoghurt
125ml/4fl oz milk
1 tablespoon sugar
½ beaten egg
1½ tablespoons vegetable oil
1½ teaspoons onion seeds
    (nigella seeds)

It you have the time, bread always tastes better if the dough is allowed to rest for at least an hour after kneading, and for naan about 6 hours is preferable.

Roti

Unleavened wholewheat flat bread

Serves 4–6

250g/9oz wholemeal flour
a pinch of salt

1 Put the flour into a bowl and mix in the salt. Pour in 125ml/4fl oz water and mix to a fairly soft dough. Turn out on to a lightly floured surface and knead for 5 minutes, until smooth and elastic, then cover with clingfilm and chill for 30 minutes.

2 Divide the dough into 12 balls. Flatten each one with your hand and then roll out into a 15cm/6 inch round.

3 Cook on preheated baking sheets in an oven preheated to 240°C/475°F/Gas Mark 9 for 3–4 minutes, or on a hot griddle for 1 minute per side (or in a hot tandoor oven for 45 seconds). When they are done, the *roti* should be slightly puffy and speckled with brown.

Chappati

Unleavened wholewheat puffed bread

Serves 4–6

250g/9oz wholemeal flour
a pinch of salt

1 Put the flour into a bowl and mix in the salt. Pour in 125ml/4fl oz water and mix to a fairly soft dough. Turn out on to a lightly floured work surface and knead for 5 minutes, then cover with clingfilm and chill for 30 minutes.

2 Divide the dough into 20 balls. Flatten each one with the palm of your hand, then roll out into a 15cm/6 inch circle.

3 Cook each *chappati* on a flat griddle over a high heat for 1 minute, then flip over and cook the other side for 2 minutes. Turn again and cook until the *chappati* puffs up.

Left A selection of Indian breads

The best breads are always freshly baked. In India a family member will bake and serve the bread while the others are eating.

Lightly fried breads are usually eaten for breakfast,

or to accompany seafood.

Poori

Deep-fried puffy bread

1 Mix the flour, salt and melted ghee together and add 100ml/3½ fl oz water to make a fairly stiff dough. Cover with clingfilm and chill for 30 minutes.

2 Divide the dough into 25 balls. Flatten each one with the palm of your hand and then roll out into a 10cm/4 inch circle.

3 Heat the oil for deep-frying over a moderate heat and fry the *poori* on both sides until they puff up. Remove from the pan and drain off excess oil in a colander.

Serves 4–6
250g/9oz wholemeal flour
a pinch of salt
1 tablespoon ghee, melted (see page 23)
vegetable oil for deep-frying

Parantha

Wholewheat flaky bread

1 Put the flour in a bowl and mix in the salt. Pour in 100ml/3½ fl oz water and bring together into a fairly stiff dough. Turn out on to a lightly floured surface and knead for 3 minutes, then wrap in clingfilm and chill for 30 minutes.

2 Divide the dough into 12 balls. Flatten each one with your hand and then roll out into a 15cm/6 inch circle. Brush with ghee and sprinkle a little flour over the top. Fold the dough into a semi-circle and then fold it again to form a triangle. Cover with clingfilm and chill for 10 minutes.

3 Roll out each triangle into a bigger triangle about 5mm/¼ inch thick. Place on preheated baking sheets and cook in an oven preheated to 240°C/475°F/Gas Mark 9 for 8–10 minutes, or on a hot griddle for 2 minutes per side (or in a hot tandoor oven for 1½–2 minutes), until the *paranthas* are golden brown.

Serves 4–6
250g/9oz wholemeal flour, plus extra for sprinkling
a pinch of salt
50g/2oz ghee (see page 23)

Chutneys

Indians enjoy eating accompaniments such as pickles, chutneys, papad, fresh green chillies and *kachumbar* (chopped raw onion and tomato) with their meals or snacks. Family recipes for pickles and chutneys are often kept secret and passed down through the generations as heirlooms, forming part of the family history.

Hinduism says a meal should have the six *rasas* (tastes) sweet, salty, bitter, pungent, sour and spicy. Chutneys can be all these things and, thus, they can help to balance the meal. They also stimulate the appetite and help digestion.

Gajar ki Chutney

Carrot chutney

Serves 4–6

500g/1lb 2oz carrots, grated
75g/3oz granulated sugar
200ml/7fl oz white vinegar
2 green cardamom pods, lightly crushed
a pinch of ground fennel seeds
$^1/_4$ teaspoon onion seeds (nigella seeds)
salt to taste

1 Put all the ingredients except the onion seeds in a pan and mix well. Bring to the boil and simmer for 1 minute.

2 Stir in the onion seeds and cook for 1 minute, then remove from the heat and leave to cool.

Pudiney ki Chutney

Mint chutney

Serves 4–6

250g/9oz coriander leaves
125g/4$^1/_2$oz mint leaves
50g/2oz yoghurt, preferably Greek yoghurt
1 tablespoon dried mango powder
1 green chilli, seeded and chopped
$^1/_2$ teaspoon finely chopped fresh ginger
1 tablespoon sugar
salt to taste

1 Put all the ingredients in a blender or food processor and mix to a smooth paste.

Nariyal ki Chutney

Coconut chutney

Serves 4–6

500g/1lb 2oz coconut, freshly grated
2 green chillies, chopped
200g/7oz roasted channa dal
1 tablespoon coconut oil
$^1/_2$ teaspoon mustard seeds
10–15 fresh curry leaves
salt to taste

1 Put the coconut, green chillies, channa dal, salt and 200ml/7fl oz water in a blender or food processor and mix to a smooth paste. Transfer to a bowl.

2 Heat the coconut oil in a small pan and add the mustard seeds. Cook for 10 seconds, until they start to splutter, then add the curry leaves and cook for 5 seconds longer. Pour this mixture on to the chutney and stir it in. Serve chilled.

One of the most popular chutneys, mango chutney can be potted and stored.

Mint chutney, however, should be eaten fresh since it is not cooked.

Aam ki Chutney

Mango chutney

Serves 4–6

500g/1lb 2oz diced mango

100g/4oz granulated sugar

1 teaspoon salt

½ teaspoon cumin seeds, roasted in a dry frying pan and then ground

2 teaspoons lemon juice

½ teaspoon finely chopped fresh ginger

½ teaspoon dried red chilli flakes

a pinch of onion seeds (nigella seeds)

2 green cardamom pods

2 cloves

1 Put all the ingredients in a pan, add 200ml/7fl oz water and bring to the boil.

2 Simmer for 5 minutes on a very low heat, then remove and leave to cool.

Tamatar ki Chutney

Tomato chutney

Serves 4–6

1 tablespoon oil

¼ teaspoon black mustard seeds

10–12 fresh curry leaves

¼ teaspoon Ginger Purée (see page 22)

¼ teaspoon Garlic Purée (see page 22)

6 tablespoons thick tomato paste

1 tablespoon vinegar

1 teaspoon sugar

salt to taste

1 Heat the oil in a pan, add the mustard seeds and sizzle for 10 seconds. Add the curry leaves and stir for 5 seconds. Add the ginger and garlic and stir for 15 seconds. Then add all the remaining ingredients and bring to the boil. Simmer for 2 minutes, then allow to cool.

Sweets

Indian sweets have a symbolic significance that goes beyond the physical act of eating them. On hearing happy news, the first reaction is, '*Muh meetha karo!*' – eat something sweet.

Most Indian *mithai* (sweets) are milk-based, using *chenna* (a type of cottage cheese) or *khoya* (reduced milk). Cereals such as wheat flour, rice lentils and semolina are also used but the most popular is *besan* (gramflour). Coconut, mango, carrots, gourd, figs, oranges, saffron, *keora* (vetiver), rose water, almonds, pistachios... anything and everything can be used for taste and flavour. Sugar toys, made by pouring sugar syrup into moulds are made for the Diwali festival in autumn and are very popular with children. They are shaped like birds and trees, or can even be in the form of Mahatma Gandhi, the father of the nation.

Then there are the nursery puddings and Club desserts, such as soufflé, bread-and-butter pudding and caramel custard, which are amongst the few culinary legacies left behind by the British Raj. At first it was a struggle to produce puddings in wood-fired ovens, but gradually, given the abundance of ingredients, successful Anglo-Indian variations appeared. Even today, old *khansamers* in army messes continue to produce light soufflés that the *burra memsahib* would have approved of.

Phirni

Almond rice pudding

1 Put the rice in a bowl, pour over 100ml/3½fl oz water and leave to soak for 30 minutes. Pour into a blender and process to a paste.

2 Put the milk in a pan and bring to the boil. Add the cardamom, reduce the heat and simmer for 5 minutes. Add the rice paste and simmer for 15 minutes, stirring constantly.

3 Stir in the sugar, almonds and raisins and simmer for 10 minutes. Pour into a bowl and leave to cool, then chill before serving.

Serves 4–6

75g/3oz basmati rice
1 litre/1¾ pints full-cream milk
2 green cardamom pods, crushed
150g/5oz granulated sugar
2 tablespoons flaked almonds
1 tablespoon raisins

Gujarat is well known for its *Shrikhand*. All festivities are celebrated with great pomp,

and feasts are served – *Shrikhand* is one of the essential sweet elements.

Shrikhand

Yoghurt with nuts

Serves 4–6

2 litres (3½ pints) skimmed
  milk
½ teaspoon set yoghurt
100g/4oz granulated sugar,
  powdered in a blender
a pinch of ground green
  cardamom
2 teaspoons crushed cashew
  nuts
1 teaspoon crushed pistachio
  nuts
1 teaspoon crushed charoli
  nuts
3 tablespoons single cream

1 Put the milk in a pan and bring to the boil, then let it cool down
to body temperature (37°C/98°F). Stir in the yoghurt, cover with
a lid and leave in a warm place overnight to set – you could wrap
the bowl in a blanket and leave it in a warm room. Alternatively,
pour it into a yoghurt-making machine and leave to set following
the manufacturer's instructions. Once it has set into yoghurt,
transfer to the fridge and leave for at least 6 hours to firm up.

2 Put the yoghurt into a piece of muslin, taking care not to
break the set curds. Tie up the ends and hang it up in a cool place
for 8–10 hours or overnight to drain off all the whey.

3 Stir in the sugar and ground cardamom and then beat the
yoghurt with a whisk until it becomes soft and fluffy, like cream
cheese. Mix in the nuts and single cream and then chill. Just
before serving, beat it again.

Rice puddings are universally eaten in South India and always on auspicious occasions.

Aam Phirni

Rice pudding with mangoes and nuts

1 Put the rice in a bowl, pour over 100ml/3½fl oz water and leave to soak for 30 minutes. Pour into a blender and process to a paste.

2 Put the milk in a pan and bring to the boil. Add the cardamom, reduce the heat and simmer for 5 minutes. Add the rice paste and simmer for 15 minutes, stirring constantly.

3 Stir in the sugar, almonds and raisins and simmer for 10 minutes. Pour into a bowl and leave to cool, then chill. Stir in the mango purée, diced mango and cashew nuts, and garnish with the silver leaf and pistachios, if using.

Serves 4–6

75g/3oz basmati rice
1 litre/1¾ pints full-cream milk
2 green cardamom pods, crushed
150g/5oz granulated sugar
2 tablespoons flaked almonds
1 tablespoon raisins
100g/4oz mango purée

150g/5oz mango, cut into 1cm/½ inch dice
2 tablespoons crushed cashew nuts
silver leaf and slivers of shelled pistachios, to garnish (optional)

Kheer

Crushed rice pudding with nuts and raisins

1 Put the rice in a bowl and pour over 250ml/8fl oz water. Leave to soak for 1 hour, then drain.

2 Put the milk in a pan, bring to the boil, then reduce the heat and simmer for 5 minutes. Add the drained rice and return to the boil. Simmer for 15 minutes, stirring constantly.

3 Add all the remaining ingredients and simmer for another 10 minutes. Serve hot or cold.

Serves 4–6

125g/4½oz basmati rice
1.5 litres (2¾ pints) skimmed milk
150g/5oz granulated sugar
2 tablespoons flaked almonds
2 tablespoons raisins
3 green cardamom pods, crushed

Left Aam Phirni

Shahi Tukra is bread pudding Hyderabadi-style.
It is usually served decorated with pure beaten silver
wrapped on sweetmeats.

Use cold toast instead of fried bread for the *Shahi Tukra*, if preferred.

Or bread rusks can also be used.

Shahi Tukra

Royal pudding

1 Cut the crusts off the bread and cut each slice into 4 triangles. Heat the oil for deep-frying and fry the bread triangles over a low heat until golden. Drain on kitchen paper and set aside.

2 Put the milk in a pan, bring to the boil and add the sugar and cardamom. Reduce the heat and simmer for 15 minutes, then remove from the heat. Soak the fried bread triangles in the milk for 10 seconds, remove with a slotted spoon and arrange in a serving dish.

3 Boil the milk, stirring occasionally, until it has reduced in volume by three-quarters. Leave to cool. Stir in the rosewater and pour the reduced milk over the fried bread triangles. Sprinkle over the nuts, garnish with the rose petals if using, and serve cold.

Serves 4–6

4 *slices of white bread, cut*
  2.5cm/1 inch thick
oil for deep-frying
2 litres/3½ pints skimmed
  milk
50g/2oz granulated sugar
2 green cardamom pods,
  crushed
¼ teaspoon rosewater
1 teaspoon crushed pistachio
  nuts
1 teaspoon crushed almonds
fresh rose petals, to garnish
  (optional)

Seviyan

Sweet vermicelli

1 Put the milk in a pan, bring to the boil and add the cardamom. Reduce the heat and simmer for 10 minutes.

2 Stir in the vermicelli and sugar and return to the boil. Simmer for 5 minutes. Serve hot or cold.

Serves 4–6

1 litre/1¾ pints milk
2 green cardamom pods,
  crushed
100g/4oz angel's hair
  vermicelli (seviyan)
150g/5oz granulated sugar

Left Shahi Tukra

Glossary

Aniseed distinctive flavouring agent, licorice-like taste.

Asafoetida dried resin available in lump form or powdered; used as a digestive spice, it has a strong aroma.

Basmati rice a long-grained, fine-textured rice, it has a nutty flavour.

Black gram beans (urad dal) protein-rich bean, with white seed.

Black salt naturally occuring salt in the form of rocks. Its powdered form is pink. It is stronger than common salt and has a distinct flavour.

Carom seeds (ajwain) small, yellowish seeds that have a sharp and piquant taste, with a fragrance similar to thyme when crushed.

Cardamom (pods and ground, green and black) a flavouring spice, it is delicately perfumed.

Cassia buds available dried or fresh, they have a flavour similar to cloves, nutmeg and cinnamon.

Channa dal yellow split peas. Roasted channa dal is channa dal which has been soaked and dry roasted. It can be eaten as a snack or used in powdered/paste form.

Charoli nuts small round nuts with a subtle flavour.

Chilli powder ground, dried red chillies; heat varies according to what type of chilli has been used.

Cinnamon (sticks or ground) the inner bark of a tree, it imparts a fragrant, slightly sweet flavour. The sticks are inedible and should be removed from the dish before eating.

Cloves (whole and ground) dried plant buds, with a strong flavour.

Coconuts/coconut oil the fruit of the coconut palm; the creamy coconut meat is pressed to make coconut oil. Coconut is high in saturated fat.

Coriander (leaves and seeds, whole and ground) the fresh leaves have a distinctive smell and flavour, and resemble flat-leafed parsley. The seeds have a milder and sweeter flavour.

Curry leaves small, bright green, shiny leaves that impart a strong curry flavour. Dried curry leaves are also available, but fresh are preferable.

Fennel seeds (whole and ground) delicately flavoured, slightly aniseedy spice.

Fenugreek leaves and seeds (whole and ground) the leaves have a flavour similar to mint. The seeds have a very strong flavour. Both are bitter in taste and should be used with care.

Garam masala spice mix (*see page* 24).

Ghee clarified butter (*see page* 23).

Ginger (fresh and dried ground) fresh ginger is a knobbly root which, when peeled, yields a fibrous pale yellow flesh. It has a spicy flavour; always try to use fresh ginger where a recipe specifies it, rather than dried ground. Dried ground ginger has an earthier quality to its flavour.

Gourds (wax, bitter, bottle, snake) long cylindrical vegetables, related to the squash family, the varieties vary in size and weight. Most have a central seed core and firm skin.

Gram flour chickpea flour.

Green chillies hot peppers, not to be confused with green peppers. The inner seeds and membrane of the chilli contain the most heat; all the flesh contains a volatile oil which results in burning of eyes or skin if care is not taken. Use with caution.

Green drumstick long, round bean-like vegetable, that tastes similar to marrow. Cut into lengths, cook and then peel.

Jaggery also known as palm sugar, sugarcane juice that is crystallised into solids. It has a strong flavour.

Lentils (red, green and yellow) rich in protein, vitamins and minerals, these pulses are extremely versatile.

Mango, dried powder (amchoor) ground dried, unripe mango, used to give a raw mango/sour flavour. Lemon or lime juice can be used as a substitute.

Mustard oil a pungently flavoured oil, extracted from mustard seeds; invaluable in pickling; when heated it has a sweetish flavour.

Mustard seeds brown or black seeds of mustard plant; have a pungent, strong flavour.

Paneer firm cottage cheese, rich in protein. Available cubed.

Pomegranate seeds available whole or powdered, they have a sweet/sour flavour.

Rosewater diluted rose essence – fragrant liquid extracted from rose petals; used in puddings and drinks.

Rice flour a thickening agent made from white rice. Different from sweet rice flour.

Saffron dried stigmas of flowers of saffron plant; strong flavouring and colouring agent. Available in strands or ground – strands are better.

Stoneflower (paththar ke phool) a kind of lichen that grows on rocks and stones. When whole, it is used with other whole spices, tied in a muslin cloth and immersed in the liquid for a slow infusion. When powdered, it should be used at the end of cooking.

Tamarind (pulp) a souring and colouring agent. Also available in blocks, dark brown in colour, resembling dates.

Tempering addition to a dish of whole or ground spices fried in very hot oil

Turmeric (ground) the ground root of a rhizome, this yellow spice is used as a flavouring and colouring agent; strongly flavoured, peppery taste.

Vetiver a mild and highly aromatic root. Also available bottled, from Asian stores, as an extract, when it is used in desserts.

Yoghurt fermented milk, indispensable in Indian cooking; it acts as a marinade, aids digestion and is invaluable in sauces.

Index

Aam ki Chutney (*Mango chutney*) 133

Aam Phirni (*Rice pudding with mangoes & nuts*) 14, 15, *136*, 137

Achari Bateyr (*Spiced whole quail*) 15, *48*, 49

Achari Spice Mix 25

Almond rice pudding (Phirni) 134

Ambotik (*Chicken in coconut & onion gravy*) 98

Ande Ka Khagina (*Scrambled eggs with chilli & coriander*) 106, *106*

apples, Mulagu-Tanni (*Mulligatawny soup*) 14, 114, *114*

apricots, Khubani Ka Murg (*Chicken with apricots*) 32, 33

aubergines

  Baghare Baingan (*Aubergines in piquant sauce*) 15, *108*, 109

  Keema Torkaari (*Lamb-stuffed vegetables*) 72, 73

  Sambhar (*Sour lentil curry with vegetables*) 14, 119

  Shobjee Jhalfarezi (*Fried vegetables*) 15, 75, *75*

  Subz Kebab (*Vegetable shasklik*) 15, 62, *63*

  Vanghi Bhaat (*Rice with aubergine*) 85

  Vanghi (*Spiced baby a ubergines*) 14, 87, *87*

Badami Kofta (*Lamb meatballs with almonds*) 44, 45

Baghare Baingan (*Aubergines in piquant sauce*) 15, *108*, 109

beans *21*

  Rajma (*Spiced kidney beans*) 15, 34, *35*

  Saag Dal (*Spinach with mung beans*) 15, 111

Bengal cuisine 65

  recipes 66-75

Bhindi Ki Kadhi (*Fried okra in sauce*) 85

Bombay cuisine 77

  recipes 78-87

Boondi 25

breads 16, 55, 127, 128-31

bulghur wheat, Haleem (*Spiced lamb with wheat*) 107

Butter, Clarified 22

Butter chicken (Murg Makhani) 43

Cabbage

  Cabbage Poriyal 15, 124, *125*

  Karamkalla (*Stir-fried spiced cabbage*) 37

carrots

  Gajar ki Chutney (*Carrot chutney*) 132

  Tarkari Biryani (*Mixed vegetable & cheese biryani*) 15, 46

Cashew Nut Paste 22

cauliflower, Tarkari Biryani (*Mixed vegetable & cheese biryani*) 15, 46

Chappati (*Unleavened wholewheat puffed bread*) 127, 129

Chat Masala Powder 23

cheese

  Malai Kebab (*Chicken kebabs*) 56, *56*

  Saag Paneer (*Spinach & cheese*) 14, 50, *51*

  Salmon Ka Tikka (*Marinated salmon*) 58

  Subz Kebab (*Vegetable shasklik*) 15, 62, *63*

  Tarkari Biryani (*Mixed vegetable & cheese biryani*) 15, 46

Chennai *see* Madras

Chholey Masala 24

chicken

  Ambotik (*Chicken in coconut & onion gravy*) 98

  Chicken Cafrael 14, *96*, 97

  Chicken Pepper Fry *120*, 121

  Chicken Tikka 59

  Chicken Vindaloo 94

  Dum Ka Murg (*Chicken in onion, yoghurt & almond gravy*) 15, *47*, 47

  Ginger Chicken 119

  Husseini Murg Masala (*Husseini chicken curry*) 68, 69

  Khubani Ka Murg (*Chicken with apricots*) 32, 33

  Malai Kebab (*Chicken kebabs*) 56

Murg Farcha (*Fried chicken*) 80, *80*

Murg Makhani (*Butter chicken*) 43

Murg Mumtaz (*Chicken in tomato, fenugreek & almond gravy*) 43

Murg Shorba (*Chicken & yoghurt soup*) 15, 40, *41*

Murg Tikka Masala (*Chicken tikka masala*) 42

Tandoori Murg (*Tandoori chicken*) 59, *59*

Chickpeas with tomatoes & chilli (Kadhai Chholey) 14, 53, *53*

Chilli Purée, Green 22

Chingri Malai Curry (*Creamy prawn curry*) 71

Chitranna (*Mango rice*) 86

chutneys 14, 15, 127, 132-3

Clarified Butter 22

coconut 140

  Ambotik (*Chicken in coconut & onion gravy*) 98

  Baghare Baingan (*Aubergines in piquant sauce*) 15, *108*, 109

  Cabbage Poriyal 15, 124, *125*

  Chingri Malai Curry (*Creamy prawn curry*) 71

  Coconut Lamb Fry (*Lamb with coconut & coriander*) 118

  Goan Prawn Curry 92, *93*

  Haleem (*Spiced lamb with wheat*) 107

  Jheenga Masala (*Lobster in the shell*) 90, *91*

  Lemon Rice 116

  Machhli Ka Saalan (*Hake in spiced coconut sauce*) 104, *105*

  Malabar Prawn Curry *122*, 123

  Mulagu-Tanni (*Mulligatawny soup*) 14, 114, *114*

  Nariyal Bhaat (*Coconut rice*) 86

  Nariyal ki Chutney (*Coconut chutney*) 132

  Nilgiri Korma (*Nilgiri lamb korma*) 14, 116, *117*

  Sambhar (*Sour lentil curry with vegetables*) 14, 119

  Shobjee Jhalfarezi (*Fried

vegetables*) 15, 75, *75*

Tamatar, Phool Gobi, Gajjar Che Saar (*Mixed vegetable curry*) 14, 15, 84, *84*

Vanghi Bhaat (*Rice with aubergine*) 85

Vanghi (*Spiced baby aubergines*) 14, 87, *87*

cod, Macher Jhol (*Fish curry*) 70

courgettes, Subz Kebab (*Vegetable shashlik*) 15, 62, *63*

cream cheese

  Malai Kebab (*Chicken kebabs*) 56, *56*

  Salmon Ka Tikka (*Marinated salmon*) 58

Creamy prawn curry (Chingri Malai Curry) 71

Crushed rice pudding with nuts & raisins (Kheer) 14, 15, 137

Curry Powder 23

Dal *20*, *21*, 140

  Dal Gosht (*Lamb & lentil curry*) *102*, 103

  Mulagu-Tanni (*Mulligatawny soup*) 14, 114, *114*

  Nariyal ki Chutney (*Coconut chutney*) 132

  Saag Dal (*Spinach with mung beans*) 15, 111

  Sambhar (*Sour lentil curry with vegetables*) 14, 119

Deep-fried puffy bread (Poori) 15, 127, 128, *130*, 131

dinner menus 15

Dum Aloo (*Whole spiced potatoes*) 15, 36

Dum Ka Murg (*Chicken in onion, yoghurt & almond gravy*) 15, 47, *47*

Eggs

  Ande Ka Khagina (*Scrambled eggs with chilli & coriander*) 106, *106*

  Keema Par Anda (*Spicy minced lamb with egg*) 81, *81*

  Murg Farcha (*Fried chicken*) 80, *80*

Fish 65
Macher Jhol (*Fish curry*) 70
Machhli Ka Saalan (*Hake in spiced coconut sauce*) 104, *105*
Salmon Ka Tikka (*Marinated salmon*) 58
Tali Machi Masala (*Fried fish*) 78, 79
Tandoori Machhi (*Tandoori trout*) 57, *57*
Fried chicken (Murg Farcha) 80, *80*
Fried fish (Tali Machi Masala) 78, 79
Fried okra in sauce (Bhindi Ki Kadhi) 85
Fried Onion Purée 22
Fried vegetables (Shobjee Jhalfarezi) 15, 75, *75*

Gajar ki Chutney (*Carrot chutney*) 132
Garam Masala 24
Garlic Purée 22
Ghee 22
Ginger Chicken 119
Ginger Purée 22
Goan cuisine 10, 89
recipes 90-9
Goan Prawn Curry 92, *93*
Goda Masala 24
gourds 140
Keema Torkaari (*Lamb-stuffed vegetables*) 72, 73
Shobjee Jhalfarezi (*Fried vegetables*) 15, 75, *75*
grains & pulses 20, *20-1*
see also individually by name e.g. rice
Green Chilli Purée 22
Gucchi Pulao (*Mushroom pilaf*) 14, *32*, 33

Hake in spiced coconut sauce (Machhli Ka Saalan) 104, *105*
Haleem (*Spiced lamb with wheat*) 107
herbs 18, *18*, 140
history, religion & regional cuisines 9-13, 16-17
see also individual regions
Husseini Murg Masala (*Husseini chicken curry*) 68, 69
Hyderabad cuisine 101
recipes 102-11

Janglee Maans (*Venison in spicy sauce*) 50, *51*
Jheenga Charchari (*Stir-fried prawns*) 14, 66, *67*
Jheenga Masala (*Lobster in the shell*) 90, *91*

Kadhai Chholey (*Chickpeas with tomatoes & chilli*) 14, 53, *53*
Karamkalla (*Stir-fried spiced cabbage*) 37
Kashmir cuisine 27
recipes 28-37
Kedgeree (Khitchuri) 65, 74, *74*
Keema Par Anda (*Spicy minced lamb with egg*) 81, *81*
Keema Torkaari (*Lamb-stuffed vegetables*) 72, 73
Kheer (*Crushed rice pudding with nuts & raisins*) 14, 15, 137
Khitchuri (*Kedgeree*) 65, 74, *74*
Khubani Ka Murg (*Chicken with apricots*) *32*, 33

Lamb
Badami Kofta (*Lamb meatballs with almonds*) 44, 45
Coconut Lamb Fry (*Lamb with coconut & coriander*) 118
Dal Gosht (*Lamb & lentil curry*) *102*, 103
Haleem (*Spiced lamb with wheat*) 107
Keema Par Anda (*Spicy minced lamb with egg*) 81, *81*
Keema Torkaari (*Lamb-stuffed vegetables*) 72, 73
Lamb Assadu (*Lamb with cinnamon & cloves*) 95, *95*
Lamb Biryani (*Lamb with fragrant basmati rice*) 15, 52
Nilgiri Korma (*Nilgiri lamb korma*) 14, 116, *117*
Qalia (*Lamb chops in yoghurt gravy*) 28, *29*
Raan Mussalam (*Roast lamb*) 60, *61*
Roganjosh (*Lamb curry*) 30
Salli Gosht (*Lamb with straw potatoes*) 82, 83
Shabdegh (*Lamb with chilli, ginger & turnips*) 31
Leavened flat bread (Naan) 14, 15, 55, 127, 128
Lemon Rice 116
lemon sole, Macher Jhol (*Fish curry*) 70
lentils *21*, 140
Dal Gosht (*Lamb & lentil curry*) *102*, 103
Khitchuri (*Kedgeree*) 65, 74, *74*

Sambhar (*Sour lentil curry with vegetables*) 14, 119
Lobster in the shell (Jheenga Masala) 90, *91*
lunch menus 14

Macher Jhol (*Fish curry*) 70
Machhli Ka Saalan (*Hake in spiced coconut sauce*) 104, *105*
Madras cuisine 9, 113
recipes 114-25
Madras Potatoes 14, 124, *125*
Malabar Prawn Curry *122*, 123
Malai Kebab (*Chicken kebabs*) 56, *56*
mangoes
Aam ki Chutney (*Mango chutney*) 133
Aam Phirni (*Rice pudding with mangoes & nuts*) 14, 15, *136*, 137
Chitranna (*Mango rice*) 86
Marinated salmon (Salmon Ka Tikka) 58
masalas & powders 17, 23, 24-5
menu planning 14-15
milk puddings 134-9
Mint chutney (Pudiney ki Chutney) 132
mixed vegetable dishes
Keema Torkaari (*Lamb-stuffed vegetables*) 72, 73
Sambhar (*Sour lentil curry with vegetables*) 14, 119
Shobjee Jhalfarezi (*Fried vegetables*) 15, 75, *75*
Subz Kebab (*Vegetable shasklik*) 15, 62, *63*
Tamatar, Phool Gobi, Gajjar Che Saar (*Mixed vegetable curry*) 14, 15, 84, *84*
Tarkari Biryani (*Mixed vegetable & cheese biryani*) 15, 46
Moghlai cuisine 12, 39
recipes 40-53
Mulagu-Tanni (*Mulligatawny soup*) 14, 114, *114*
Mumbai *see* Bombay
mung beans *21*
Saag Dal (*Spinach with mung beans*) 15, 111
Murg Farcha (*Fried chicken*) 80, *80*
Murg Makhani (*Butter chicken*) 43
Murg Mumtaz (*Chicken in tomato, fenugreek & almond gravy*) 43
Murg Shorba (*Chicken & yoghurt soup*) 15, 40, *41*
Murg Tikka Masala (*Chicken tikka

masala*) 42
mushrooms
Gucchi Pulao (*Mushroom pilaf*) 14, *32*, 33
Subz Kebab (*Vegetable shasklik*) 15, 62, *63*
Tarkari Biryani (*Mixed vegetable & cheese biryani*) 15, 46

Naan (*Leavened flat bread*) 14, 15, 55, 127, 128
Nariyal Bhaat (*Coconut rice*) 86
Nariyal ki Chutney (*Coconut chutney*) 132
Nilgiri Korma (*Nilgiri lamb korma*) 14, 116, *117*
non-vegetarian menus 14, 15

Okra
Bhindi Ki Kadhi (*Fried okra in sauce*) 85
Sambhar (*Sour lentil curry with vegetables*) 14, 119
onions
Ambotik (*Chicken in coconut & onion gravy*) 98
Dal Gosht (*Lamb & lentil curry*) *102*, 103
Dum Ka Murg (*Chicken in onion, yoghurt & almond gravy*) 15, 47, *47*
Fried Onion Purée 22
Raw Onion Purée 22

Panch Phoran Spice Mix 25
paneer 140
Saag Paneer (*Spinach & cheese*) 14, 50, *51*
Subz Kebab (*Vegetable shashlik*) 15, 62, *63*
Tarkari Biryani (*Mixed vegetable & cheese biryani*) 15, 46
Parantha (*Wholewheat flaky bread*) 14, 15, 55, 127, 128, 131
peas, Tarkari Biryani (*Mixed vegetable & cheese biryani*) 15, 46
peppers
Husseini Murg Masala (*Husseini chicken curry*) 68, 69
Keema Torkaari (*Lamb-stuffed vegetables*) 72, 73
Subz Kebab (*Vegetable shashlik*) 15, 62, *63*
Phirni (*Almond rice pudding*) 134
pomfret, Tali Machi Masala (*Fried fish*) 78, 79
Poori (*Deep-fried puffy bread*) 15,

127, 128, *130*, 131
potatoes
   Chicken Vindaloo 94
   Dum Aloo (*Whole spiced potatoes*) 15, 36
   Madras Potatoes 14, 124, *125*
   Qalia (*Lamb chops in yoghurt gravy*) 28
   Salli Gosht (*Lamb with straw potatoes*) *82*, 83
   Shobjee Jhalfarezi (*Fried vegetables*) 15, *75*, 75
   Tarkari Biryani (*Mixed vegetable & cheese biryani*) 15, 46
prawns
   Chingri Malai Curry (*Creamy prawn curry*) 71
   Goan Prawn Curry *92*, 93
   Jheenga Charchari (*Stir-fried prawns*) 14, 66, *67*
   Malabar Prawn Curry *122*, 123
   Prawn Balchao (*Spiced prawns*) 15, *99*, 99
   Pudiney ki Chutney (*Mint chutney*) 132
pulses & grains 20, *20-1*
   see also individually by name e.g. rice
pumpkin
   Sambhar (*Sour lentil curry with vegetables*) 14, 119
   Shobjee Jhalfarezi (*Fried vegetables*) 15, *75*, 75
purées 22

Qalia (*Lamb chops in yoghurt gravy*) 28, *29*
quail, Achari Bateyr (*Spiced whole quail*) 15, *48*, 49

Raan Mussalam (*Roast lamb*) 60, *61*
Rajma (*Spiced kidney beans*) 15, 34, *35*
Raw Onion Purée 22
red kidney beans *21*
   Rajma (*Spiced kidney beans*) 15, 34, *35*
regions of India (history, religion & cuisines) 9-13, 16-17
   see also individual regions
rice *20*, 65, 140
   Aam Phirni (*Rice pudding with mangoes & nuts*) 14, 15, *136*, 137
   Chitranna (*Mango rice*) 86
   Gucchi Pulao (*Mushroom pilaf*) 14, *32*, 33

Kheer (*Crushed rice pudding with nuts & raisins*) 14, 15, 137
Khitchuri (*Kedgeree*) 65, 74, *74*
Lamb Biryani (*Lamb with fragrant basmati rice*) 15, 52
Lemon Rice 116
Nariyal Bhaat (*Coconut rice*) 86
Phirni (*Almond rice pudding*) 134
Sesame Rice 14, 123
Tamatar Waale Chaawal (*Tomato rice*) 110
Tarkari Biryani (*Mixed vegetable & cheese biryani*) 15, 46
Vanghi Bhaat (*Rice with aubergine*) 85
Roast lamb (Raan Mussalam) 60, *61*
Roganjosh (*Lamb curry*) 30
Roti (*Unleavened wholewheat flat bread*) 15, 55, 127, 128, 129
Royal pudding (Shahi Tukra) 15, *138*, 139

Saag Dal (*Spinach with mung beans*) 15, 111
Saag Paneer (*Spinach & cheese*) 14, 50, *51*
Salli Gosht (*Lamb with straw potatoes*) *82*, 83
Salmon Ka Tikka (*Marinated salmon*) 58
Sambhar (*Sour lentil curry with vegetables*) 14, 119
Sambhar Powder 25
Scrambled eggs with chilli & coriander (Ande Ka Khagina) 106, *106*
Sesame Rice 14, 123
Seviyan (*Sweet vermicelli*) 14, 139
Shabdegh 31
Shahi Tukra (*Royal pudding*) 15, *138*, 139
Shobjee Jhalfarezi (*Fried vegetables*) 15, *75*, 75
Shrikhand (*Yoghurt with nuts*) 14, *135*, 135
sole, Macher Jhol (*Fish curry*) 70
soups
   Mulagu-Tanni (*Mulligatawny soup*) 14, 114, *114*
   Murg Shorba (*Chicken & yoghurt soup*) 15, 40, *41*
   Thakkali Rassam (*Thin tomato soup*) 15, 115
Sour lentil curry with vegetables (Sambhar) 14, 119
Spiced baby aubergines (Vanghi) 14, *87*, 87

Spiced kidney beans (Rajma) 15, 34, *35*
Spiced lamb with wheat (Haleem) 107
Spiced prawns (Prawn Balchao) 15, *99*, 99
Spiced whole quail (Achari Bateyr) 15, *48*, 49
spices 17, 18, *18-19*, 127, 140
   mixes, masalas & powders 17, 23, 24-5
Spicy minced lamb with egg (Keema Par Anda) 81, *81*
spinach
   Saag Dal (*Spinach with mung beans*) 15, 111
   Saag Paneer (*Spinach & cheese*) 14, 50, *51*
split peas *20*, 140
   Dal Gosht (*Lamb & lentil curry*) *102*, 103
   Mulagu-Tanni (*Mulligatawny soup*) 14, 114, *114*
Stir-fried prawns (Jheenga Charchari) 14, 66, *67*
Stir-fried spiced cabbage (Karamkalla) 37
Subz Kebab (*Vegetable shashlik*) 15, 62, *63*
Sweet vermicelli (Seviyan) 14, 139
sweets 55, 127, 134-9

Tali Machi Masala (*Fried fish*) 78, 79
Tamatar, Phool Gobi, Gajjar Che Saar (*Mixed vegetable curry*) 14, 15, 84, *84*
Tamatar ki Chutney (*Tomato chutney*) 133
Tamatar Waale Chaawal (*Tomato rice*) 110
Tandoor cooking 16, 55, 127
   recipes 56-63
Tandoori Machhi (*Tandoori trout*) 57, *57*
Tandoori Murg (*Tandoori chicken*) 59, *59*
Tarkari Biryani (*Mixed vegetable & cheese biryani*) 15, 46
Thakkali Rassam (*Thin tomato soup*) 15, 115
tomatoes
   Kadhai Chholey (*Chickpeas with tomatoes & chilli*) 14, 53, *53*
   Murg Makhani (*Butter chicken*) 43
   Murg Mumtaz (*Chicken in tomato, fenugreek & almond*

gravy) 43
   Tamatar ki Chutney (*Tomato chutney*) 133
   Tamatar Waale Chaawal (*Tomato rice*) 110
   Thakkali Rassam (*Thin tomato soup*) 15, 115
trout, Tandoori Machhi (*Tandoori trout*) 57, *57*
turnips, Shabdegh (*Lamb with chilli, ginger & turnips*) 31

Unleavened wholewheat flat bread (Roti) 15, 55, 127, 128, 129
Unleavened wholewheat puffed bread (Chappati) 127, 129

Vanghi (*Spiced baby aubergines*) 14, *87*, 87
Vanghi Bhaat (*Rice with aubergine*) 85
vegetables *see* individual vegetables by name; mixed vegetable dishes
vegetarian menus 14, 15
Venison in spicy sauce (Janglee Maans) 50, *51*
vermicelli, Seviyan (*Sweet vermicelli*) 14, 139

Wheat, Haleem (*Spiced lamb with wheat*) 107
Whole spiced potatoes (Dum Aloo) 15, 36
Wholewheat flaky bread (Parantha) 14, 15, 55, 127, 128, 131

Yoghurt 140
   Bhindi Ki Kadhi (*Fried okra in sauce*) 85
   Dum Ka Murg (*Chicken in onion, yoghurt & almond gravy*) 15, 47, *47*
   Murg Shorba (*Chicken & yoghurt soup*) 15, 40, *41*
   Qalia (*Lamb chops in yoghurt gravy*) 28
   Shrikhand (*Yoghurt with nuts*) 14, 135, *135*

Copyright

First published in 2001 by HarperCollins*Publishers*.

Recipe text copyright © G K Noon 2001
Narrative text copyright © Mohini Kent 2001
Food photographs copyright © G K Noon 2001
Reportage photographs pp76, 100, 26, 28, 30, 31, 34 copyright
© Travel Ink 2001
All other reportage photographs copyright © Richard Lewisohn 2001
Portraits of G K Noon and Chefs copyright © G K Noon/Graham Trott 2001

G K Noon reserves the moral right to be identified as the author of the Work.

FOOD STYLING, ART DIRECTION, AND DESIGN CONCEPT:
New Crane Communications Ltd
Food photographs: Philip Webb
Styling: Helen Trent

FOR HARPERCOLLINS*PUBLISHERS*:
COMMISSIONING EDITOR: Barbara Dixon
DESIGN MANAGER: Mabel Chan
DESIGNER: Mark Stevens
INDEXER: Susan Bosanko

A catalogue record for this book is available from the British Library.

ISBN 0 00 711675 6

Printed and bound by The Bath Press